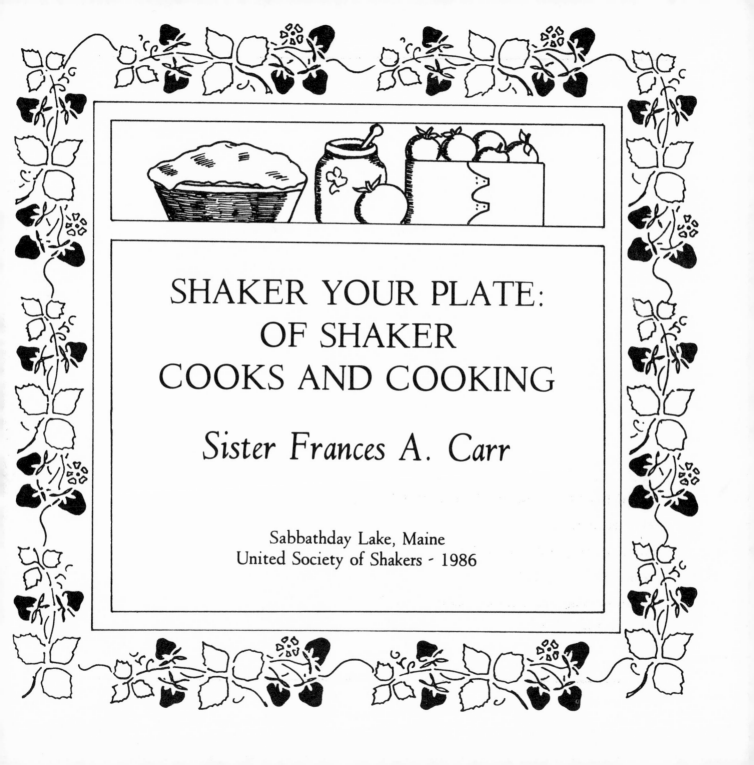

SHAKER YOUR PLATE: OF SHAKER COOKS AND COOKING

Sister Frances A. Carr

Sabbathday Lake, Maine
United Society of Shakers - 1986

SHAKER YOUR PLATE

DEDICATION

To Sister Mildred and Brother Ted, whose lives are daily reminders that man does not live by bread alone.

ACKNOWLEDGMENTS

This little book owes much to many people. I am especially appreciative of the work of Genie Belletete of Amesbury, Massachusetts, who has graced its pages with her delightful illustrations so much in the Shaker tradition. Special thanks is due, too, to Brother Arnold for many hours of typing. The book would never have appeared without Brother Ted's encouragement freely lent over a period of several years, in which I was all too ready to abandon the projected work. He is also to be thanked for the enormous burden of reading and editing, which he has so freely undertaken. Last, but certainly not least, I should like to thank all of my brothers and sisters in the Shaker community at Sabbathday Lake, not only for their patience and concern, but also for having allowed me to test all of the recipes on them.

Sister Frances A. Carr
Sabbathday Lake, Maine
S S. Mary and Martha 1985

FOREWORD
(A Thank Offering)

Shaker cookery, like everything Shaker-designed or Shaker-created, is traditionally simple and functional. If it is gourmet gastronomy you seek, or some rare epicurean dainty, forget it. You won't find exotics among these recipes. What you *will* find are simple directions for the preparation of time-tested comestibles, each conceived with loving care, to be of delicious taste and a wholesome, satisfying nature. When you get right down to it, isn't that what good food is all about? The Shakers, bless them, have known it for over a hundred years.

Martin Dibner

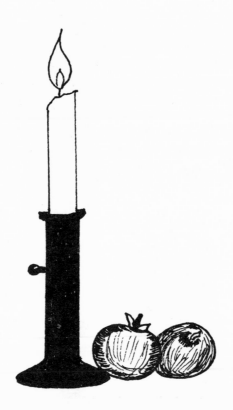

CONTENTS

SHAKER YOUR PLATE

INTRODUCTION
TO BOOK

This is not intended as an all inclusive Shaker cookbook. Certainly there is no need or want for another cookbook, Shaker or otherwise; they seem to emanate from every museum or historical society, from every church and women's club. This is good, as the exchange of recipes has long been a custom in this country and especially in the New England area. Someone recently said that, other than the Bible, cookbooks sell faster than any other publication. This is easy to understand when we consider the importance of breaking bread together. Be it in one's own kitchen or dining room, at a church supper or grange hall, nothing seems to bring people closer together than the act of sharing food. We here at Sabbathday Lake find that some of our favorite scripture selections have to do with that sharing of food. I have always thought that the first real picnic is that written of by St. Matthew when we read of that huge assemblage of people who had come to hear Jesus preach at the end of the day find themselves with not

enough food. What a wonderful scene is conjured up by that description of those early miracles in which the few loaves of bread and the fishes are multiplied to feed thousands. We here at this Shaker Village in Maine love picnics, and to me that has always seemed like one of the greatest, with the sea spread out before and that mass of humans all over the green hillside.

Again that account of the disciples arriving on shore after a night of fishing to find a breakfast of fish and bread toasting on the coals holds great appeal. No doubt this same appeal of food is what has caused the public to be so anxious for cookbooks, especially those pertaining to a special way of life.

Over the years, friends who have visited this community, especially those who have broken bread with us, have asked that I make some of my favorite recipes available to the world. This is what this little volume is; a collection of recipes used here at

Sabbathday Lake over the years and passed along to those of us who continue on in the tradition of Shaker cooking.

What is Shaker cooking? Basically it is plain, wholesome food well prepared. This book is not intended for the sophisticated palate, nor for the gourmet (although many people have referred to some of the dishes as being gourmet). It is not meant for those who enjoy eating in expensive restaurants where one may find lobster dishes, steaks and prime rib of beef. Shakers in Maine did not have this type of food. It is intended for those people who enjoy simple foods painstakingly prepared. In my thirty-odd years of cooking in the Shaker kitchen, I have used recipes passed on by Shaker cooks who taught me as a child, and whose recipes have come down through the years. It is only natural, of course, for each individual cook to experiment and to develop her own style of cooking, to add her own touch; this I have done. It is also a natural development that with the passing of years, other recipes of the day would come into use.

This little collection includes a few dishes of which some of those early Shaker cooks would never have heard. They were not privileged to have many of the convenience ingredients which we take so much for granted available to them. (I am sure they would have loved using such ingredients.) It has been difficult for me to decide which recipes to put into this little volume with so many available. Sabbathday Lake is, after all, into its third century of feeding the hungry.

One could go on for years, but that is not my intent. After much discussion with the entire community, as well as with some friends from the world, we have chosen those recipes most used by us and most often asked for by good friends.

Sometimes the recipes have never been written out, but exist only in my head. In these cases I have attempted to be as accurate as possible in putting the ingredients and amounts down on paper. I have never taken a course in home economics in a formal sense. Because most of my recipes are intended to feed a large amount of people, it has been especially difficult for me to reduce them to the size of the average family. If readers encounter any problem in this respect, I hope that they will feel free to contact me. Most of these recipes originated here in Maine at either Alfred or Sabbathday Lake. Neither community has had a reputation for the style of food often found in other Shaker cookbooks. Rather theirs was and is the simple, down-to-earth cooking of rural Maine.

Over the past twenty-five years, the arrival of Brothers Ted, Arnold and Wayne has introduced a more sophisticated trend in the cooking now done in the community. Brother Ted's Swedish Chicken and Brother Arnold's Beef Stroganoff are typical examples. The Swedish Chicken is one of our favorite picnic meals; it travels well. The Beef Stroganoff is a rarity usually served on very special occasions, a birthday or spiritual anniversary. Brother Wayne's applesauce cake with rose water frosting is a general favorite, too.

It is impossible to write Shaker recipes without relating a few facts about the cooks, so I will tell a little about those individuals who played a role in my experience over the years as a Shaker cook and deaconess. It would be impossible to write about everyone over a period of forty-odd years, so it is those special people with whom I worked most closely, and who for one reason or another greatly influenced that part of my Shaker experience gained in the kitchen.

SISTER ETHEL PEACOCK

My very first introduction to the Shaker kitchen was under the care and charge of Sister Ethel Peacock. It was my good fortune to begin my venture into its realms of wonder and delight under her charge. She had come from the Alfred Society when that family moved to Sabbathday Lake. Her warmth and goodness to the younger members of the now large Community soon earned her the name of "Grandmother," a name which she carried to her death. A large woman with snowy white hair and blue eyes, she was physically the epitome of a grandmother to the many young people living at the Village who did not have a grandmother near. Soon after the move from Alfred, Sister Ethel became one of the head cooks at the Community. While she always claimed not to care for cooking, her chocolate pudding cake and baking powder biscuits were favorites with the Community.

Sister Ethel was also during this period in charge of the Shaker Museum. At that time it was a small museum with only a few visitors daily. She was, it seemed, frequently called away from her work in the kitchen to take someone over to the museum. This never bothered her; on the contrary, it delighted her. She loved people much more than she did stoves, pots and pans, and she was a charming hostess. Her many friends all over the country who were first introduced to Shakerism through her role as museum hostess were myriad. I have often felt that one of the reasons I have developed into a cook was due to the many times that Sister Ethel would be called away in the middle of preparing some dish, and would tell me to take over until she returned. If one learns from experience, then I certainly had the experience at an early age. I was a special favorite of Sister Ethel's and the feeling was mutual. I have many happy memories of helping her as a little girl. She was in charge of the Dairy, and as a small child I would assist her. My duty was to wash the pails and help clean up the dairy, but she would often allow me to mould the butter into long rolls for the Community's use. She made me feel very important and needed, two very important aspects of a child's growth. Sister Ethel was one of the first persons I had ever seen taping Shaker chairs. It was my duty on summer afternoons to assist her in pulling the tapes through the seats of the chairs. One of her favorite expressions was that she "needed a pair of hands," and I was often that pair of hands.

ELDRESS PRUDENCE STICKNEY

During the time that I was a novice in the Shaker kitchen, Eldress Prudence was known as the "kitchen angel," a term which came about because of her habit of coming into the kitchen each noontime to wash up the dishes that had collected over the morning. These were mostly pots, pans and cooking dishes. Eldress Prudence was in her early 80's during this time and was, of course, the spiritual head of the Sisterhood. It was a wonderful gift which she shared with the kitchen Sisters and younger girls.

There were 4 people working a two-week shift at that time. Had it not been for her kind volunteerism, it might not have been otherwise possible for some of the teenagers to be with Eldress Prudence and to have the opportunity to share in her knowledge of long ago Shaker days. She had come to the North Family at Poland Hill in 1864 as a child of 4. I realize now how great a lesson in humility she was giving us. Here is the head of the Shaker Community washing the dirty pots and pans in the midst of such hustle and bustle. As most people who cook on a large scale know, the hour just before serving the dinner is a tense time, especially in hot weather when air conditioning in a Shaker kitchen was unknown. The arch kettles were also much in use during the summer months. They created a lot of hot steam, and when people were tired and tempers a bit frayed, her presence served to lighten everyone's load and to bring a feeling of calm into the busyness of a large kitchen at noontime.

Eldress Prudence had been a cook in her younger days and still continued to make special dishes. For some reason it was her wish to make oyster stew (in the large arch kettle) whenever we had it. She also enjoyed making Shaker stewed tomatoes, as well as Shaker fish and egg, which was also another of her specialties. It may be that this had some influence on my taste perception for I was very fond of her. At any rate, those dishes have never tasted the same to me as when Eldress Prudence made them. The kitchen was always a prime source of interest to her and up to the time she could no longer leave her room, she was always buying some extra special pot or pan, or some little device to make work easier or to encourage those people working in the kitchen. She presented a rare picture. She was a tiny person, not five feet tall, and probably never weighing more than 90 pounds. Her dresses were floor length and she had 2 aprons which I especially remember. One was gray and white check, and the other was purple and white check. The aprons were also floor length so that just the tips of her shiny, black-buttoned shoes showed as she scurried around the kitchen and dining room.

Each fall the making of mince meat was a regular production. This was another area in which Eldress Prudence even in her last years continued to be in charge. Its was a huge task involving a great deal of preparation prior to the actual cooking. All of the able people would assemble in the sauce room to prepare the ingredients, and then Eldress Prudence with an assistant (for many years my older sister, Kate) would cook the mince meat. This was done in the old arch kettles which may still be seen in the sauce room and are still useable.

A heavy mixture, it required a lot of stirring, which is what my sister did. Eldress Prudence, standing on tip-toe, would supervise. After the cooking was completed, it was stored in canning jars and put away for the winter. The aroma filled the Sisters' Shop with a never to be forgotten scent, and no pie since then has had the flavor of Eldress Prudence's mince meat.

Another production which involved all of the able-bodied people in the community was the canning of chicken. For years, as long as I can remember and certainly for many years predating my coming to the community, the Shakers at Sabbathday Lake had a thriving egg business. The large hen house was taken down in the 1950's. As was the case with so many industries, lack of people able to carry on the work, as well as the increase in grain prices made it impossible to continue with the hen and egg business. During the peak of this industry many hundreds of dozens of eggs were sold in greater Portland where we had steady customers, and each Monday (regardless of weather) the trip to town with cases of fresh eggs was part of the day.

Little chicks were purchased each spring and raised up to become egg bearing hens. As the new hens matured, the older hens who were no longer peak bearers were killed off to make room for the new. For some reason that I do not know, a Monday was always chosen as the day to prepare the hens for canning. Probably this was because we were more rested after the Lord's Day and better able to face this task which was greatly disliked by almost all of the community. The wash room at the Sisters' Shop was readied with layers of newspaper and a fire was made in the great arch kettle to insure plenty of boiling water. Once the hens had been butchered (usually by hired men) they were brought in by the bushel and quickly dipped into the boiling water. The younger members and young people would then go to work plucking the feathers out. This was known as "picking" a hen. As soon as a hen had been picked, the Sisters would open it up and clean it out. It was exciting to find completely formed eggs in some of the hens. It was not uncommon to prepare as many as 75 to 100 hens a day.

The next day they were cut into pieces and boiled in preparation for putting them up in glass jars. There was something very special about the flavor of home preserved chicken. I have never experienced that delicious flavor in any chicken dish since.

Eldress Prudence and Sister Elsie McCool would supervise the canning of the chicken, and the whole community, or those who could be spared and were able to work took part. I realize now that even though it was terribly distasteful to me and to all of us at the time, it did have a lot of fun associated with it. With all of the older Sisters there we heard many fascinating tales of what used to be.

During the last 4 or 5 years of her life, Eldress Prudence would eat a very early and light supper. Although her strength had not diminished noticeably and she continued to put in a full day of work, she seemed to enjoy being in her room early. There she spent the evening knitting or working on her vast correspondence. At 5:00 each evening one could find her sitting in the little Shaker chair at the small curly maple Shaker table just inside and to the right of the back door of the kitchen.

She nearly always had a bran muffin and applesauce with a little tea. One molasses cookie now and then completed her meal. Always a lover of animals her favorite collie dog, Jack, always knew when she would be having her supper and somehow always managed to creep into the kitchen and lie very still by her chair. We all soon learned not to notice that he was there. Once having had the last bite, he would disappear and not enter the kitchen again until the following evening when his beloved friend would have her supper.

BROTHER DELMER WILSON

"Shaker your plate" has become a popular expression in the so-called "world of Shaker," yet few people probably realize that the first time Shakers here at Sabbathday Lake heard the expression was when Brother Delmer used it many years ago.

When I came to the Shakers 47 years ago, as a very small child, meals were eaten in silence except for an occasional request. Brother Delmer sat at what was known then and is still known as the Brothers' table. He sat at the end facing the dining room and the other seven places were occupied by young men and small boys. Like all Believers Brother Delmer was very opposed to waste of any kind, and so it was not unusual to hear suddenly emanating from his place the gruff and curt remark, "Shaker your plate." Brother Delmer himself was so meticulous about this aspect of saving that he would even take his finger and pick up all the crumbs which might have fallen around his place. Of course this might have been his way of cleaning up around his spot, for he was a very fastidious person both in dress and surroundings. The old-time Shaker neatness manifested itself in Brother Delmer. He was one of the few Shakers who never shared work generally regarded as belonging to the opposite sex. To my knowledge he never boiled the proverbial cup of tea. Coming to the Shakers at the early age of 8 years, he was placed under the care of Sister Amanda Stickney (Eldress Prudence Stickney's natural sister), who mothered the young boy with much love and tenderness. Probably no crown prince was cared for with such thoughtfulness. He loved to tell stories of how she never let him wash or iron a single piece of clothing. This attitude must have carried over into the world of cooking because no one remembers him cooking or washing a dish. Although I have no recipes to include here from Brother Delmer, there are reasons why he should be represented in the Shaker cookbook. Not only does he deserve a place for his "Shaker your plate," which is half of this book's title, but for the many little things that he taught me about setting a table. Brother Delmer was as particular about his table settings as he was about everything he did. For many years he was the only Brother eating at the Brothers' table. Under the table by his plate he had installed an electric bell connected to the kitchen. On more than one occasion we would be summoned to the dining room by the bell to have him tell us that he wanted the butter removed and a cleaner portion brought in. There were probably crumbs on the butter plate to which he objected. Serving dishes of food must never be too full, nor have spilled over the edge. While at the same time it may have seemed difficult for us to be called into the dining room and to be reprimanded by Brother Delmer, it was, in retrospect, responsible for us setting a good table.

Brother Delmer maintained a strict regimen concerning his diet and weight. One wondered how he functioned on such a small amount of food. Perhaps the fact that he enjoyed a few pieces of candy in the late afternoon helped. He would become upset if he thought any of the young people or Sisters were overeating. It was not uncommon to look up and see him scowling at an over zealous eater. One always knew that after the meal he would approach the individual and speak of it. Needless to say, those who sat facing Brother Delmer seemed to have less appetite than those who could not be seen by him.

Every morning except for Sunday when the hired men did not work on the farm, Brother Delmer would come into the kitchen at twenty minutes of 10 (he seldom varied so much as a minute) and would have 2 Ritz crackers and a cup of instant coffee with lots of milk and sugar. I never knew him to vary from this routine. He would eat very slowly and relax completely. Then, just before 10:00, he would go back to the farm where he worked along with his hired help for the rest of the day. Brother Delmer was there to meet the men when they arrived for work at 7:30, and did not leave work until they left at 4:30. This continued to be his habit until just 2 or 3 years before his death when he began to take things a little easy.

One very human aspect of Brother Delmer's day which delighted the rest of his Shaker family was his love of the comic strip *Nancy*. He always subscribed to the *Portland Press Herald* and it was his custom to leave the dining room each noon early enough to be able to read the comic strip and report back to his men at 1:00 on what happened to Nancy. I think that this was one of the down-to-earth traits which endeared him to the hired help. During the many years that Brother Delmer ran the farm we never saw pork served in the community. We did keep hogs (rather than compost heaps) and wonderful hogs they were, but each fall when it came time to slaughter, the hired men and their respective families received the bonus of hams, bacon, chops and roasts. All of the meat was given to them much to the dismay of some of those cooking in the community kitchen. Brother Delmer firmly believed that pork caused cancer. Although he never, to my knowledge, and I am sure of this, ate a morsel of pork or smoked a cigarette, Brother Delmer died of lung cancer in his 89th year. It should be noted that for years Brother Delmer raised prize beef cattle as well as dairy cows. His reputation as a farmer was widespread. One cannot go far at the Shaker Community at Sabbathday Lake without encountering the marks of Brother Delmer, for he was a very talented person. Perhaps best known for the thousands of carriers he made, he was also an electrician, plumber, farmer and artist, along with other talents too numerous to mention here.

I always enjoyed a wonderful personal friendsip with Brother Delmer. Another young person of my age and myself were dubbed the "heavenly twins" by him. I am grateful for the association of the years with Brother Delmer and for the opportunity of helping to care for him during his last weeks of life. Although a severe Shaker Brother for most of his life, he mellowed into a kindly, grandfatherly sort of person. I will never hear the words, "Shaker your plate," without thinking of that venerable Shaker who would often startle the stillness of the community dining room with those words.

SISTER MARIE BURGESS

Sister Marie began to work in the community kitchen rather later than most people. She came to Sabbathday Lake as a young woman of 19, and was placed at the Trustees' office to assist in the very busy and profitable Shaker candy industry, which at the time was headed by Sister Jennie Mathers.

When Sister Marie was no longer needed to help with the Office kitchen work, she came to work in the family or community kitchen. Sister Marie had had little opportunity to cook, so she came into the kitchen knowing very little about its challenges. She loves to tell that I taught her all she knows. If this is true, then I am very pleased with my pupil!

When I was learning to cook there were always four people working in the kitchen for a two-week period. By the time Sister Marie began to cook, it was just her and myself. She soon mastered the art of bread and pastry making. While cooking is not something she especially enjoys, her breads, pies and biscuits have become favorites with all who know them.

I would find it difficult indeed to work in the kitchen without Sister Marie. She knows what I am going to do almost before I mention it, and is never at a loss in helping to prepare whatever we may be having. She is truly my right hand, and much of the success of my cooking is due in great part to her assistance.

Her excellence as a bread maker, both white and dark varieties, attests to her dedication and patience in a trade which is so essential to the happiness of a family. Truly bread is the staff of life, and this community has long been sustained by Sister Marie's good breads.

SISTER MINNIE GREENE

Sister Minnie Greene came to the Sabbathday Lake Society when the Alfred, Maine Society closed and its members all moved to Sabbathday Lake. She had come to Alfred as a little girl of 11. Sister Minnie was soon adapting her skills in the kitchen of her new home and over the years progressed to the role of head baker. Her specialties were and still are in the bakery department She has become famous for her cookies, especially the molasses ones which have gone far and near. The recipe for them is certainly one of the most often requested by friends and visitors alike. She is also well known for the pot holders which she has turned out by the thousands over the years. Whenever we have a large gathering you can be sure that there will be large plates of her delicious jumble or molasses cookies in evidence.

SISTER ELIZABETH DUNN

Sister Elizabeth Dunn was one of the regular Shaker cooks from the time I first knew her in 1937 until she passed away in 1981. She was first the baker, in charge of making bread, pastry, cookies and the like.

When Sister Della Haskell retired from kitchen work due to ill health, Sister Elizabeth took over as one of the head cooks. It was never one of her favorite occupations, but she certainly made many good things that were other people's favorites. Among her specialties were the biscuits she really enjoyed making, lemon pie, cherry pie, which she made especially for the younger people, and her very fine squash pie. No matter who happened to be the cook at Thanksgiving she was always asked to come in and make the squash pie. This she delighted to do. Another favorite which she prepared exceptionally well was shepherd pie.

Sister Elizabeth came to the Sabbathday Lake Shakers as a girl of 14, and was placed under the care of Sister Iona Sedgeley. During her early adult years she was in charge of the hen house. During those years, the Society regularly sold eggs to customers in the Portland area, so the care and management of the eggs and chickens was no small responsibility. Many times we have seen Sister Elizabeth with the help of young people going to the hen house on snowshoes when the snow was too deep for ordinary travel. She was a conscientious keeper of the hen house.

She had learned hand sewing skills under Sister Iona's tutelage and would use quiet times in the kitchen to turn out handmade items for the Gift Shop. Whenever we make any of her special recipes she is vividly remembered and missed by her family.

NON COOKS

When the Alfred Shakers moved to Sabbathday Lake there were 21 new arrivals here. With the exception of a few older people, Eldress Harriet Coolbroth, Sister Eva Libby, Sister Eliza Jeffers, Elder Henry Green and Brother Stephen Gowen, they were for the most part healthy and in their prime. I guess it was a natural thing to have many of the younger Sisters take over in the kitchen at Sabbathday Lake where, apparently, help was badly needed. I do not remember any Sabbathday Lake Sister working in the kitchen after the Alfred people arrived, with the exception of Sister Elizabeth.

With 60 or more people to cook for the kitchen was a busy place, filled with time consuming work. The kitchen work was set up into blocks of two weeks for four people. The two who did most of the cooking and supervising were known as the head cook and the baker. The other two were usually young sisters, whose duties included preparing vegetables for cooking, as well as washing pots and pans and keeping the kitchen clean. The younger people were taught as they worked, thus allowing them to grow into greater responsibility in both cooking and baking. Another Sister with a little girl, usually 8 to 10 years of age, would do the dishes in the dining room. The finer dishes and silverware were always washed there. The larger serving dishes and cooking pots and pans were done in the kitchen.

It was not uncommon to have Eldress Prudence and Sister Iona, an older Sister whose chief duties were making the famous Shaker cloaks and working on poplarware, come into the kitchen to make a dish that they were somehow known for; Shaker fish and egg, Shaker stewed tomato, or their famed oyster stew.

During the 1930's and '40's Sister Jennie Mathers had been turning out the famous Shaker candies. Sisters Marie Burgess and Minnie Greene assisted in this work, and Sister Mildred Barker was Sister Jennie's assistant. For years Sister Mildred hand-dipped the chocolates turned out in the basement of the Trustees' Office. When Sister Jennie passed away, Sister Mildred continued to manage the candy business, adding many varieties. In addition to her famous mints, she made hundreds of pounds of fudge, stuffed dates, peanut clusters and, during the height of the candy industry, was turning out 31 varieties of chocolates. What wonderful candy it was! By 1965 the price of chocolate, the lack of workers and an ailing back forced Sister Mildred to give up the candy industry, though she still makes stuffed dates and fudge occasionally, but not on the scale she once did.

During these years Sister Mildred also had charge of the young people (sometimes as many as 12 at one time), so she did not, of course, spend much time in the Shaker kitchen. She did, and still continues to make her doughnuts, the recipe for which appears in this book. Her creamed potato is still a favorite and we enjoy this special old time dish about once a month.

On those days when the chicken canning was going on Sister Iona Sedgley, who had been severely lamed during her adult life, would go into the kitchen so as to allow the younger and more able ones to help with the canning. Once during the coffee or tea break Sister Iona fixed egg salad sandwiches. She could not understand why her choice did not go over well. Surrounded by chickens and eggs as we were, it was not something that any of us had an appetite for.

Although Sister Elsie McCool did not work in the kitchen during these years, she was in charge of the preserving, a herculean task in itself. The story of the preserving would easily fill another book, so I will not go into much of it here other than to say that it was very exciting work. The young people would be up in the family gardens during the day harvesting vegetables and fruits. A pick-up truck would drive up to the huge double doors of the preserving area where all members of the family who were able were waiting to peel and prepare the produce for the jars. In the sauce room the arch kettles would be steaming, ready for the huge amounts of boiling water, so much a part of this process. Once the gardens began to yield their produce, this work could go on for several days each week for many weeks. In the autumn it was fruits from the orchards - pears, plums, peaches and of course apples which occupied our attention.

Sister Elsie was also in charge of the pickling for the use of the community. Sister Mildred was in charge of making pickles and jellies for sale, not only in our gift shop, but for the many trips which the Sisters took abroad selling fancy work and other Shaker items made for the world.

DAIRY

With all of the emphasis paid today to the dangers of cholesterol and fats, one wonders why this never seemed to be a problem with the Shakers of fifty years ago. Certainly butter, cream and good rich milk were used regularly and no one seemed to suffer from their consumption. On the contrary, good health and long years seemed to be the blessing of those Believers. I often think back to those days, especially when making a recipe which always seemed to be especially delicious due to the cream and butter no longer so readily available. I have not tasted Shaker fish and egg such as that made by Eldress Prudence in over thirty-five years. The Shaker stewed tomatoes also had a flavor which is difficult to emulate today. The oyster stew, made in the large arch kettle, was mainly good rich milk with plenty of butter. Today's stews lack this flavor, and even if the cream and butter were easily available, we would eat it with a guilty conscience knowing of the cholesterol involved.

In writing about Sister Ethel I mentioned the dairy work which was carried on in the little dairy across the hall from the community kitchen and dining room. The milk brought in each afternoon around five o'clock would be stored in the ice box until ready to churn. Brother Delmer raised prize jerseys and wonderfully rich milk was always available. One of the younger persons in the kitchen had the duty of straining the milk as it came from the barn. A special sterilized straining cloth was used. It was attached to a strainer which in turn was placed over the milk pans. I remember eight shiny milk pans being in constant use daily. The milk was then set in the refrigerator until the next day, then the heavy cream would rise to the top. What fun it was to skim this cream off with a little ladle used especially and only for this purpose. There was always plenty of cream left in the milk to ensure a good rich milk for drinking and with ten or more small children and about a dozen teenagers the milk was put to good use. Cottage cheese was a daily part of the dairying process. The cheese was made by the cook who happened to be doing kitchen duty at the time. Sister Mildred still thinks fondly of and looks back with yearning on the "good old homemade cottage cheese." Sister Ethel shared dairy duties with Sister Olive Dobson. It was my good fortune (though I did not always think so at the time) to help Sister Ethel in molding the long rolls of butter and placing them in the long scooped out wooden butter tray. A great deal of meticulous care was given to the dairy industry. I do not recall that the Community ever sold butter commercially as they did eggs, but often a visitor to the Community would leave with a package containing a rich yellow roll of freshly made butter.

The dairy was equipped with an electric churn (at least in my day), clear running cold water, a black iron sink, and a disposable drain in the floor. Directly

outside the Brothers' waiting room and adjacent to the kitchen was a long bench made of wood with wooden spokes coming up like fingers. Eight pails hung on these wooden spikes and were never used for any purpose other than for carrying milk from the barn. Often on a rainy day, the sound of rain beating against the up-ended bottoms of the milk pails would drown out normal conversation. Today the former dairy is used as the Community's print shop.

On Memorial Day in the year 1955, the cow barn, complete with silo, was struck by lightning and destroyed by fire. Fortunately there were no animals in the barn at the time, but surely a lot of Shakeriana went up in flames. It was difficult to see the tragic look on Brother Delmer's face as he watched this edifice where so many hours of labor and of happiness had been spent go so quickly. The fire threatened the entire Village, and Memorial Day of 1955 will always be remembered as an unhappy example of what can happen when nature runs amok. The huge granite foundations still remain in the barn field, a reminder to those of us who remember the barn when it was home to Daisy, Rosie and Buttercup, a few of Brother Delmer's favorite bovine friends.

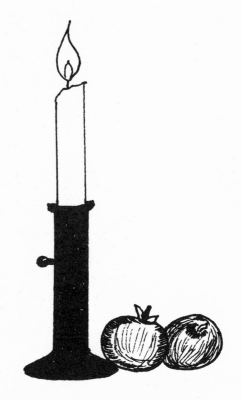

HERBS

It is a pretty well known fact that for many years the Shakers were among the largest herb growers in the country. They were the first to raise and package botanicals for sale. In the year 1864 the Society here issued its first printed catalogue of *Herbs, Roots, Barks and Powders.* There were 155 items offered at that time. They were shipped all over the United States and Canada. This industry, like so many others in which the Shakers were engaged, met stiff competition from the industrial world. As new priorities arose the herb business faded from the prominence it had once known. From the closing of the medicinal herb department in 1911 through the 1950's, very little herb activity was carried on here. By 1962 the country was going through a resurgence of interest in more natural lifestyles. More and more young people were returning to rural areas and an interest in natural foods was especially strong. People were beginning to discover both the beneficial aspects of herbs as well as the pleasure they brought to one's culinary sense. Brother Ted immediately felt that this was the time to re-establish the herbal industry once so much a part of nearly every Shaker Community's existence. Our first attempts were minor indeed. A plot of mint transplanted from the shores of Sabbathday Lake was the beginning of a small garden. Incidentally, if you are thinking of starting an herb garden, mint is the easiest to grow.

You just can't kill it. One does not need good soil for the herbs. They seem to thrive in poor soil so that anyone regardless of space can grow them. Little by little we added to the herb garden. We began looking for and discovered many herbs growing wild on the property. No doubt they were left over from the once thriving industry which once encompassed acres here at Shaker Village. We still find such things as Pipsissewa in the old granite quarry and other relative rarities in the fields and woods.

Herbs offer a means by which one may make a meal attractive to look at, as well as good to eat. I will always remember the advice of the first Shaker cook under whom I worked. She asked me to picture in my mind a meal consisting of white fish, mashed potato and cauliflower, followed by tapioca pudding as a dessert. "Pretty washed out and apparently bland, isn't it?" she queried. "Then, try this mental picture: white fish baked and topped with a sprinkling of tarragon or parsley, carrots served with a butter and dill sauce, and instead of mashed potatoes, small boiled potatoes rolled in melted butter and chervil. The tapioca pudding is then highly acceptable, because there is enough color now to offset the whiteness of the original whole." It is truly amazing how the addition of colorful herbs can make a special dinner from what might otherwise have been a very mediocre meal. One doesn't have to serve expensive foods to create an appetizing meal. The addition of herbs alone can make a tremendous difference.

In talking of herbs and the benefits of using them long ago, the Shakers said, "herbs stimulate the appetite. They give character to food and add charm and variety to ordinary dishes." Herbs are not a luxury. If used correctly they go far. Since the time of the earliest Greeks, Egyptians and Mesopotamians they have belonged to the diet of king and commoner, rich and poor.

Those who have been using herbs for some time are aware of the importance of keeping them away from both light and heat. Beginners must remember never to keep herbs stored on the top of the stove. Also it is not a good practice to keep them too long, as they do tend to lose flavor after a prolonged period of sitting on one's shelves. One of the most important things to remember about herbs is not to overdo their use. In the earliest stages of learning to use herbs - when one is still experimenting as it were - one may easily go overboard. I will never forget when I first became a cook at the village, I was reading a good deal about cooking and about the fun of making things different by adding unusual seasonings and flavorings. Once while preparing the Thanksgiving dinner I though that I would be different, so I added a great deal of Worcestershire Sauce to the interior of the turkey. It was awful! Not only did it taste horrible, but it looked dreadful. That poor turkey had an interior the color of pitch, and was most unappetizing. It would have been bad enough had this been an ordinary dinner, but a Thanksgiving dinner! I was devastated

to say the least. I learned there and then to be careful and not overdo. It is much better to wish that you had added just a little bit more, than to wish that you could take away some seasoning after the fact.

A pretty good rule of thumb to follow is to begin by using about a third of a teaspoon of a dried herb, or a teaspoon of a fresh herb in a dish for 4 people. Dried herbs are about 3 times as strong as fresh. I usually add herbs to my cooking toward the end. In seasoning cold foods, however, the longer they are combined, the better the flavoring grows. We might add that one should be particularly sparing in the use of herbs in cold food, for the potentially subtle flavoring may become overwhelmed if too much is used and the dish left to cool for too long. I could go on and on about the fun of cooking with herbs, but let me mention a few herb mixtures which we have concocted here at Shaker Village. It is sometimes difficult to know which herb to use in which dish, so we are going to provide you with a sample sheet that will tell you not only a little about that, but about the mixtures which we compound here as well. The mixtures, all of which are best sellers among our herbal products, are as follows: *Bouquet Garni*, which is excellent on tomato dishes and with red meats; *Fines Herbes*, which I use in chowders and with fish and poultry. Or perhaps I might put it better this way. In using *Bouquet Garni* I think red or orange, red meats, tomato dishes, Italian food and the like. With *Fines Herbes* I think white - fish, fowl and milk-based dishes,

chowders in particular. A dear old doctor friend of mine who had come to this country from France once told me that *Fines Herbes* turned an ordinary fish chowder into a gourmet dish. He may have exaggerated a bit, but I always use it and am pleased with the results. *Herbal Bouquet*, which is our third mixture, is especially good on vegetables.

The first herbs we sold were packaged in small glass bottles and were sold in our Gift Shop. It soon became apparent that Shaker herbs were once again going to be popular, and at this time we began to enlarge the gardens by purchasing from other herb farms seedlings and plants. By the late 70's we had approximately 10 acres planted to herbs. In 1973 we changed our small bottles into tin cans which are made especially for us. In the 1860's the tins in which herbs were sold were of exactly this type. We attempted to find a tin as much like that as possible. At that time we also began in earnest our mail order business.

SHAKER CULINARY HERBS
Suggested Uses

1. ANISE SEED   A few seeds perk up the taste of many a soup. Use in applesauce in place of cinnamon or nutmeg. Good in cheese spreads; also breads, cakes and cookies.

2. BASIL   Great in tomato dishes. Enhances eggplant, peas, green beans, zucchini and cucumbers. Use in macaroni and cheese.

3. BOUQUET GARNI   Our heartiest herbal mixture. A fine additive for rich soups and stews. Good in all tomato dishes and salads.

4. CARAWAY SEED   In rye and black breads. Add to cakes, puddings, cookies and apple dishes of all kinds. Also in boiled cabbage and pickled beets.

5. CELERY LEAVES   In soups, stews and stuffing.

6. CHERVIL   Called the "gourmet parsley." Best known for use in salads, but it enhances soups, especially sorrel or spinach soup; and adds flavor to fish, eggs, meats or vegetables.

7. CORIANDER SEED   In rich cakes, custards and jellies. Imparts a wonderful spiciness to sausage and red meats. A tasty addition to pickles and beet salads.

8. DILL   In salads. Excellent in seafood salads, especially shrimp. Use in many pickle recipes. Can be used as a garnish or freshener in place of parsley.

9. DILL SEED   Add a few seeds to yogurt, cucumbers, green beans and other vegetables, and to soups, stews, tomato juice and cottage cheese.

10. FENNEL SEED — On breads, rolls, cakes and cookies before baking. Add to baked apples. Use in roasting and stewing meats. Very good on fish and in seafood casseroles.

11. FINES HERBES — In fish or corn chowder, a few minutes before serving. On vegetables just as serving them. In any egg dish or cheese casserole.

12. HERBAL BOUQUET — In stews and other meat dishes.

13. MARIGOLD — "The poor man's saffron." In salads, broths and soups. Great with rice.

14. MARJORAM — "Herb of grace." In salads. Lends flavor to all meats, fish, eggs and most vegetables. Also makes a good tea, and can be used as a breath freshener.

15. OREGANO — In all tomato dishes and sauces. Goes well with most meats, salads and vegetables. Use it an herb butter to pour over cooked vegetables.

16. PARSLEY — Garnish on vegetables, meats and fish. In butter or boiled potatoes.

17. ROSEMARY — A tangy herb to flavor beef, veal, pork, lamb, poultry, soups, stuffings, sauces and salad dressings.

18. SAGE — To flavor sausages, fowl, pork and cheeses. In stuffing for poultry and veal. In sauces. Use with parsley to temper the pungency of the sage. An excellent and healthful tea.

19. SAVORY — In egg dishes, most meats, fowl and green salads. In butter it makes a tangy spread.

20. TARRAGON — Chicken, tomato juice, on eggs (sparingly). It is strong and aromatic, so be delicate with it and use it toward the end of cooking.

21. THYME — Chicken, fish and most soups and chowders. A little in butter to pour over vegetables. Great with lamb.

ORCHARDS

In addition to Brother Delmer giving voice to the "Shaker your plate" of our title and teaching the young people in unexpected and not always appreciated ways, he contributed a great deal to the kitchens of the Sabbathday Lake Shakers through his wonderful orchards and dairy barn. Although there was from the earliest days a small assortment of apple trees at Shaker Village, Brother Delmer began in 1912 to set out many young trees not only to make it possible for the community to have plenty of fruit, but also with the intent of entering a commercial business. Although the MacIntosh and Cortland along with both Red and Yellow Delicious were the commonly sought-after apples, many of the old and almost extinct varieties were planted. The Pippen, Winter Banana, Rhode Island Greening, Jonathan, Ben Davis, Baldwin and Red Astrachan were among those begun in the early days of the century.

By the time I came to work in the kitchen, a few of the older varieties had lost their popularity commercially. This is unfortunate as they really had a flavor lacking in the MacIntosh and Cortland, delicious though they may be. Because of the abundance of apples, many recipes in this book will use that fruit. Just below the apple orchard situated on a slope directly behind the Meeting House are several sour cherry trees. These have borne bountifully for years. We usually have an abundance not only for fresh cherry desserts, but also to put in the freezer for the long days of winter when fruit is at a premium in Maine. A few peach and pear trees also situated in the same area as the cherry trees provide us with their special treats. By the end of autumn the long-used Shaker cupboards in the cellar under the kitchen are filled with jars of canned pears. To my mind no other process of preserving fruit compares with the good quality of that home canned in mason jars.

Until 1945 a plum orchard behind the Sisters' Shop bore many varieties of that fruit. During Sister Elsie's days of overseeing the preserving, not only were many jars of plums preserved, but delicious jellies and jams were also put up. For some unknown reason Brother Delmer had the plum orchard cut down and the area turned into a field. Today the only fruit to be found on the east side of the village is a large plot of rhubarb and a solitary pear tree.

The apple orchards which were a delight to Brother Delmer soon became well known and it was not uncommon to have the Maine State Pomological Society hold its annual meeting in this beautiful spot. The orchard overlooks the entire village. It is high on a hill and as one drives from either north or south approaching the village, its beauty is visible. In late May the apple blossoms provide a beauty hard to surpass. The white and pink blooms are so thick they

seem to cast a light over the area, and the scent of over 2400 apple trees heavily laden with blossoms wafts down throughout the village, permeating all with its sweetness.

There is a special beauty to the orchard in the cold days of winter, too. The starkness of its branches reaching towards the sky and silhouetted against a flaming red winter sunset is often a reason for cars to draw off from Route 26 and behold its beauty.

The apple orchard was probably Brother Delmer's chief source of pride and delight during the last 20 years of his life. It was his habit to drive up to the orchard in his old pick-up at sunset and sit for a while contemplating the beauty of this spot which held so many of his own hopes and dreams spread out over the years of toil. He used to love to watch the little foxes come out of their dens and scurry around with their little babies. The noise of the highway which passes through the village is always muted in the orchard and deer would often come out hesitantly, feeling that there was a human in sight. Brother Delmer would be so still that often these animals would pass within a few feet of him.

The apple industry was a lucrative one and brought a great deal of attention to Shaker Village. When it became apparent that Brother Delmer would not be able to continue to maintain the orchard, it was leased out to a local orchardist with the understanding that

the Shakers could always have as many apples as they desired. It is still one of our favorite places of retreat. Up there on that hill away from the noise and bustle of the world it is easy to feel the spirit of Brother Delmer, and to visualize him at the day's end looking over the place he loved so well.

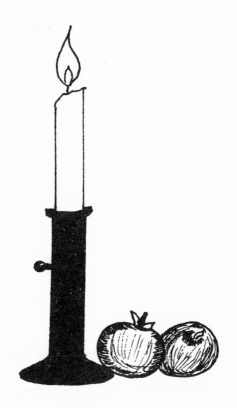

RECIPES

FATHER JAMES' PRAYER

"I pray God would make us thankful for the necessaries of life, but above all things, make us thankful for the gospel."

Father James Whittaker
Shirley, Massachusetts, 1782

SOUPS

CHEESY TOMATO SOUP

1 cup onions, finely chopped
¼ cup butter or margarine
4 cups tomato puree
2 cups water
5 cups grated cheddar cheese
3 cups sour cream

In a medium soup kettle melt butter. Saute the onions until transparent. Add in tomatoes, water and cheese. Heat over medium heat until the cheese is melted and the soup is hot. Stir in the sour cream. Heat through but do not allow to boil. Serves 8.

TOMATO DILL SOUP

1 teaspoon butter or margarine
1 teaspoon flour
2½ cups tomato puree
½ teaspoon baking soda
2 teaspoons Shaker Dill
Salt to taste
5 cups hot milk
½ cup sour cream (*optional*)

In a medium size soup kettle melt the butter. Stir in the flour and cook for several minutes. Add tomato puree, dill and salt. Stir in the baking soda. Simmer for 30 minutes. Heat milk and slowly stir into the sour cream. Add milk mixture to tomato mixture. Heat, stirring constantly, until hot.

HEARTY BEEF AND VEGETABLE SOUP

3 to 4 pound soup bone or beef shank
1 teaspoon salt
1 bay leaf
½ cup diced celery
1½ cups diced potatoes
1½ cups diced carrots
½ cup diced turnip
3 medium onions, chopped into large chunks

In large kettle combine bone or shank, salt, bay leaf, celery and 1½ cups water. Bring to a boil and reduce heat to simmer. Cover and cook for 1½ hours or until the meat is tender.

Remove shanks and allow them to cool slightly. Skim fat off surface and cut meat from bones into small pieces approximately 1 inch. Set meat aside.

In the stock combine all vegetables and bring to a boil. Reduce heat and allow to simmer for approximately 20 minutes or until potatoes, carrots and turnips are almost tender. Add meat and continue simmering until all the vegetables are tender. Do not allow the meat to boil as it will grow stringy. Just before serving add ½ teaspoon Shaker Bouquet Garni and serve very hot with herb biscuits.

For several years we have had a crock pot or slow cooker, truly wonderful things. I now always cook the meat bone or shank in the crock pot the night before. When the bone is first put into the pot with onions and seasonings I turn the cooker on high for approximately 1 hour and then reduce the heat to medium and cook all night. In the morning the meat is fork tender and so flavorful. Sometimes if this is to be the main meal and I want a real hearty soup I will add a pound of stew meat to the bone, especially if the bone doesn't have a good amount of meat on it. I cook the vegetables on the stove as usual, as vegetables tend to be longer cooking and turn mushy in a crock pot. Just be sure to remove the meat from the stock and add only towards the end of the cooking time.

Sister Mildred is especially fond of this soup so I always try to make enough to have some left over which I freeze and have on those few occasions when she isn't feeling well.

SISTER FRANCES' CORN CHOWDER

½ cup chopped onion (*I prefer large chunks*)
½ cup diced potatoes
1 heaping teaspoon Shaker Celery Leaves
1 8-ounce can kernel corn (*some people prefer cream style, I like the whole kernel*)
2 cups boiling water (*if using canned corn use the liquid from the can as part of the 2 cups*)
Salt & pepper to taste
1 cup evaporated milk
1 heaping tablespoon butter or margarine
¼ teaspoon Shaker Fines Herbes

In boiling water cook the potato and onion until done. Do not overcook. Add corn and celery leaves. Allow to come just to boiling point. Reduce heat and add milk, butter and fines herbes. Serve very hot with saltines, biscuits or hot breads.

OLD FASHIONED CHICKEN SOUP

3 pound tender chicken
1 teaspoon salt (*optional*)
¼ teaspoon Shaker Fines Herbes
1½ cups diced potatoes
1 cup diced carrots
4 medium onions, chopped

Wash chicken as usual. Place in large kettle and cover with approximately 5 cups of water. Allow to simmer until chicken is tender. Allow to cool. Remove meat from the bones. I usually cook the whole chicken though most people prefer to cut it up before cooking. When the stock has cooled skim off as much fat as possible. Cook the vegetables in the stock which has been heated to the boiling point and then simmer until vegetables are tender. Ten minutes or so before the soup is ready add the chicken meat which has been cut up into fairly large pieces. Add the fines herbes just before serving. Be sure the soup is very hot.

I always cook the chicken in the same way that I do the beef in the beef soup recipe.

SISTER FRANCES' VEGETABLE SOUP

3 cups turnip
4 cups carrots
4 potatoes
2 cups cabbage
2 large onions
2-3 bullion cubes
¼ teaspoon Shaker Oregano
¼ teaspoon Shaker Parsley

Cut the turnip, carrots, potatoes and onions into small pieces. Finely shred the cabbage. Place the vegetables, bullion cubes, oregano and parsley into a crock pot or a kettle. Add water to cover and cook on low for a few hours. If you are working during the day place the crock pot on low and leave all day. All the flavors and aromas of this soup come out. It is delicious.

Sister Frances concocted this little recipe just recently. One of the Brethren cannot eat red meat but he loves soup, so she took a look around the kitchen and cut up these vegetables and a few hours later, voila, heaven in a bowl!

SPLIT PEA SOUP

3½ cups boiling water
1 ham bone *(better with plenty of meat and fat)*
1½ cups yellow split peas *(many prefer green, but we like yellow)*
1 teaspoon salt
¼ teaspoon pepper
1 onion, chopped

In a fairly large pot, so as to have room for slow cooking and swelling, combine all of the above ingredients. Cook slowly for 2½ to 3 hours. We use the pressure cooker as it cuts down on the cooking time. Remove the bone from the stock and cut all the ham away from the bone. If you have any extra ham, it would be good to cut it into small pieces and add to the soup. Just before serving add 1 heaping tablespoon of butter or margarine and ¼ teaspoon Shaker Chervil to soup and allow to blend thoroughly. Heat to very hot and serve with Sister Marie's corn bread.

We usually have this during the winter for a supper meal. Sometimes we serve corn muffins in place of the corn bread.

SALADS

AUTUMN SALAD

2 avocados
4 apples
1 cucumber
2 medium onions, thinly sliced
½ cup diced celery

Peel, stone and slice avocados. Core and slice the apples, but do not peel. Slice cucumber without peeling. Thinly slice onions and separate into rings. Combine all ingredients.

DRESSING

1 cup plain yogurt
¼ cup French dressing
1 teaspoon celery seed

Combine all ingredients together. Mix well. Add to the above salad. Garnish with fresh parsley.

Each year just before the holidays we usually receive a wonderful box of avocados from our friends, the Browns, of Glendora, California. This is a superb gift and is put to good use.

APPLE AVOCADO SALAD

2 tart red apples, Cortland preferred
2 tablespoons lemon juice
1 cup sliced celery
¼ cup chopped pecans
½ cup miniature marshmallows
½ cup pineapple tidbits
Salt and pepper to taste
½ cup mayonnaise
2 or 3 avocados

Dice apples and sprinkle with lemon juice. Combine celery, nuts, pineapple, marshmallows and drained apple cubes. Toss lightly with mayonnaise. Cut avocados in halves. Remove stones and fill with apple mixture. Serve on lettuce. You may serve extra mayonnaise in a separate dish.

CUCUMBER SALAD

2 cucumbers
½ onion
½ cup sour cream
½ cup Shaker Mint Vinegar
½ teaspoon salt
¼ teaspoon pepper
2 tablespoons sugar
¼ teaspoon mustard

Make sure that your cucumbers are fresh and tender. Peel one but leave the other unpeeled. Slice very fine. Sprinkle with salt and let stand 3 minutes. This removes any bitter taste of the skin. Mix dressing of sour cream, vinegar and seasonings together. Combine well. Pour over cucumbers and serve at once.

APPLE AND TUNA SALAD

1 7-ounce can tuna (*I prefer tuna packed in water rather than oil*)
2 red apples
½ cup sliced celery
½ cup salted peanuts
½ cup mayonnaise
½ cup sour cream
¼ teaspoon Shaker Fines Herbes

Drain tuna and flake. Core and dice apples, but do not peel. Combine tuna, celery, apples and nuts. Combine mayonnaise and sour cream. Combine all ingredients and serve on lettuce. Sprinkle the fines herbes on top of salad.

SHELLED BEAN SALAD

3 small green onions
Shelled beans or string beans
Cheesecloth bag consisting of:
   ⅛ teaspoon Shaker Thyme
   ⅛ teaspoon Shaker Sage
   1/3 small onion
   1/3 bay leaf
French dressing
2 teaspoons chives
2 teaspoons Shaker Chervil
2 teaspoons Shaker Parsley

When you cook the beans add the cheesecloth bag of herbs to the pot. When the beans are done, discard the cheesecloth bag and drain the beans. While the beans are still warm, pour over dressing, onions and herbs. Allow to cool and serve on lettuce.

HERBED APPLE SALAD

2 cups diced apples, unpeeled
½ cup raisins
1 cup pineapple tidbits
1 teaspoon Shaker Marjoram
¼ cup mayonnaise
2 tablespoons orange juice

Toss apples, raisins and pineapple together. Mix mayonnaise with marjoram and orange juice. Add to fruit and toss lightly. Serve on lettuce leaf.

TUNA RICE SALAD

1½ cups cooked rice
¼ cup French dressing
¾ cup mayonnaise
¼ teaspoon salt (*optional*)
1 tablespoon finely chopped onion
½ teaspoon celery seed
½ cup diced celery
1 hard boiled egg, chopped
1 cup flaked tuna

Add the French dressing to rice while rice is hot. Allow rice to cool and then add the remaining ingredients. Toss lightly. Chill at least 1 hour before serving. Any left over peas may be added to the salad.

MOLDED CHICKEN SALAD

2 cups diced chicken
1 cup diced celery
½ cup chopped pecans
1 cup mayonnaise
1 cup cream, whipped
1 tablespoon unflavored gelatin
¼ cup cold water

Soak gelatin in cold water. Dissolve over hot water. Combine mayonnaise and cream. Add cooled gelatin, chicken, nuts and celery. Combine well and pour into mold. We find that it works well to use individual custard cups instead of a mold. When serving, turn out onto a leaf of lettuce. Garnish with half an olive or sliced hard boiled egg.

Thanks to a very good friend in Virginia, we receive each year a large box of pecans right from his tree. How fortunate we are to have such a friend!

DILL AND COTTAGE CHEESE SALAD

2 tablespoons Shaker Dill
2 tablespoons mayonnaise or salad dressing
1 cup grated carrot
2 tablespoons grated onion
2 cups cottage cheese

Combine the dill and mayonnaise and let stand for approximately 2 hours. This may be mixed well in advance and kept in the refrigerator tightly covered and ready for use. Toss other ingredients together and add the mayonnaise. Combine thoroughly but lightly.

Sister Mildred always laments the passing of the home-made cottage cheese. To her it had a very special flavor not to be found in the commercial brands.

SISTER DELLA'S FAVORITE FRUIT SALAD

3 cups ripe pears, cut into large pieces
3 cups peaches, cut into large pieces
3 large apples (*your choice, although Red Delicious is our favorite*), cut into thin slices
1 cup grapes
2 large oranges, cut into chunks
1 cup mayonnaise
1 cup sweet cream
Lettuce
1 teaspoon Shaker Caraway Seed

Mix mayonnaise and cream together. Blend the fruit into mixture. Blend fruit lightly so that it is all covered and yet is not mushy. Sprinkle caraway over top. Serve on lettuce.

HOT CHICKEN SALAD

2 cups cooked chicken
1 cup chopped celery
½ cup chopped pecans
½ teaspoon salt
1 10-ounce can cream of chicken soup
2 teaspoons chopped onion
½ teaspoon Shaker Tarragon
2 cups potato chips
½ cup mayonnaise

Mix all ingredients together. Place into a 1½ quart casserole dish. Before baking, top with crumbled potato chips. Bake in a 350° oven for 30 minutes or until it is bubbling.

BREADS

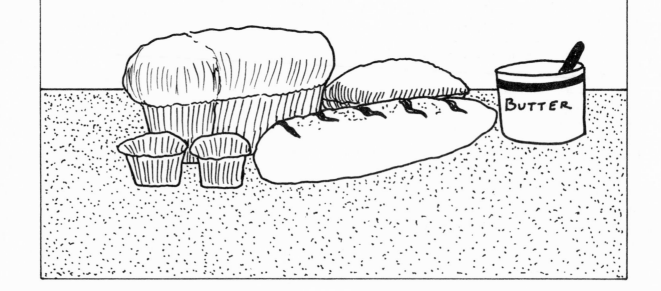

SISTER MARIE'S WHOLE WHEAT BREAD

1 cup milk
2 tablespoons sugar
2 teaspoons salt
¼ cup butter or margarine
½ cup molasses
1½ cups warm water (temperature of 105°-115°)
2 packages dry active yeast
2½ cups sifted all-purpose flour
5 cups *unsifted* whole wheat flour
2 tablespoons melted butter or margerine

Heat milk until bubbles form around the pan, remove from heat. Add the sugar, salt, butter and molasses. Stir until butter melts. In a large bowl sprinkle the yeast over water and stir until dissolved. Stir in the milk mixture. Add all-purpose flour and 2½ cups of whole wheat flour. Beat with wooden spoon (if you have one) until smooth, about 4 minutes. Gradually add remaining whole wheat flour, mixing in the last of it with your hand, until the dough leaves the sides of the bowl.

Turn dough out onto a lightly floured board and allow to rest for 10 minutes. Knead until smooth, about 10 or 12 minutes. Kneading is very important to good bread so do not neglect it. Place dough in a greased bowl and turn the dough so as to bring the greased side up. Cover with a light towel and let rise in a warm place away from drafts until dough doubles in bulk, about 1¼ hours. A good test is to poke 2 fingers into the dough and if the indentation remains the dough is ready. Punch down dough with hands (this is a good way to let off steam about something troublesome). Turn dough out onto lightly floured board, divide in half and shape each half into a smooth ball. Let rest for 10 minutes. Shape each portion into a loaf and place in lightly greased 9 x 5 loaf pans. Cover with a towel and let rise in warm place until double in bulk or until the dough reaches the tops of the pans. This takes approximately 1½ hours.

Preheat oven to 400°. Bake loaves 40-45 minutes. The tops should be browned and sound hollow when rapped with knuckles. Remove bread from pans immediately and let it cool.

This bread freezes well, so if two loaves are too much, put one loaf, well wrapped, into the freezer.

This bread is sold at our Christmas fair by the dozens. It is very popular and it makes great toast when it is day old.

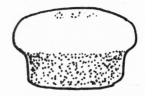

67

PUMPKIN BREAD

1 cup sugar
1 cup brown sugar
1 cup oil
3 cups pumpkin, cooked and drained
1 teaspoon salt
1 teaspoon cinnamon
½ teaspoon ground cloves
½ teaspoon ginger
½ teaspoon nutmeg
4 teaspoons baking soda
4 cups flour
1 cup chopped nuts (*optional*)
1 cup raisins (*optional*)

Combine the sugars, flour, salt, spices, baking soda, nuts and raisins together. Mix thoroughly. Add the oil and pumpkin. Mix well. Spoon into 2 loaf tins. Bake at 350° for 1 hour or until done.

CHEESE & SAGE BREAD

½ cup shortening
1/3 cup sugar
1 egg, beaten
1 cup grated sharp cheese
2 cups flour
3 teaspoons baking powder
1 tablespoon dried Shaker Sage
¾ cup milk

Cream shortening and sugar. Add beaten egg and then the cheese. Sift the flour with baking powder. Add to the shortening mixture. Mix in the sage. Gradually stir in the milk to desired consistency. Turn into greased pan and brush the top with melted butter. Bake in a 350° oven for 1 hour.

This bread is especially good with chicken for sandwiches.

SISTER MARIE'S GRAHAM BREAD

4½ cups all-purpose flour
2½ cups stone ground graham flour
2 packages active dry yeast
1 tablespoon salt
1/3 cup honey
3 tablespoons soft butter or margarine
2½ cups hot tap water

Sift the all-purpose flour into a bowl. Add the undissolved yeast and salt. Mix well to be sure that it is thoroughly blended. Add honey, hot water and butter. Again blend well. You may use an electric mixer, but Sister Marie prefers to mix by hand with the aid of a wooden spoon. Add the graham flour. Mix well. Turn out onto floured board. Knead 5-10 minutes until the dough is smooth and elastic. Cover with plastic wrap and then a towel. Let dough rest 20 minutes on the board. Punch down, divide in half and shape each half into a loaf of whatever shape you like. It may be round or oblong. Flatten loaves slightly. Place in greased loaf tins, or if you make round loaves, place them in greased 8″ pie tins. Cover pans lightly with plastic wrap. Refrigerate 2 to 24 hours. When ready to bake, remove from refrigerator and uncover. Let stand 10 minutes while you preheat oven to 400°. Bake for 40-45 minutes or until done. Do not underbake. We find that if you use a lower rack in the oven we get better results. If the crust becomes too brown during baking, cover with foil. Remove pans immediately and cool on racks. Yields 2 loaves.

Points to remember: Bread must stay in the refrigerator for the minimum of 2 hours and no longer than the stated 24 hours. It is also important to thoroughly mix and knead the dough.

CRANBERRY BREAD

2 cups flour
½ teaspoon salt
½ teaspoon baking soda
1 cup sugar
1½ teaspoons baking powder
Juice and grated rind of 1 orange
1 egg, beaten
2 tablespoons melted shortening
1 cup cranberries
½ cup broken nut meats

Sift dry ingredients together into a large bowl. Put

juice and grated rind of orange in measuring cup and add enough boiling water to make ¾ cup. Add to dry mixture. Add egg and melted shortening and mix just enough to moisten flour mixture. Add cranberries and nut meats. Bake in a greased loaf pan 45-50 minutes at 325°. Store 24 hours before cutting. Yields one loaf.

COFFEE CAN BREAD

4 cups flour
1 package yeast
½ cup warm water
½ cup milk
½ cup butter
¼ cup sugar
1 teaspoon salt
¾ cups raisins
2 eggs, beaten
3 teaspoons cinnamon

Combine yeast with the warm water and set aside. Heat the milk, butter, sugar and salt together. Heat until the butter melts. Cool to lukewarm and add the yeast mixture. Combine with 2 cups of flour and the cinnamon. Add the raisins and beaten eggs. Gradually add the remaining flour. Oil 2 coffee cans. Divide mixture in half. Place mixture in cans and allow to rise for 1 hour. Bake in a 375° oven for 35 minutes.

This bread has delighted many friends and relatives lucky enough to receive some as presents during the holidays.

OUR FAVORITE
CORN BREAD

1 cup yellow corn meal
1 cup all-purpose flour
¼ cup sugar (this is optional - if you object to sugar for any
    reason, it may be left out with no problem)
4 teaspoons baking powder
Dash of salt, approximately ½ teaspoon or less
1 cup sweet milk
1 egg
¼ cup vegetable shortening

Combine corn meal, flour, sugar, baking powder and
salt. Add milk, egg and shortening to the above
mixture. Beat until fairly smooth. Bake in a greased 8"
square pan in a preheated oven at 425° for 20-25
minutes.

*This recipe may also be used for muffins by cooking the above
mixture in muffin tins. We prefer the muffins, as they seem
less crumby. Both ways are good. They are excellent with soups
or chowders.*

SISTER ELIZABETH'S
BISCUITS

4 cups bread flour
3 teaspoons baking powder
8 level tablespoons shortening
1 teaspoon salt
2 tablespoons sugar
2 cups milk

Combine flour, baking powder, salt and sugar
together. Mix well. Cut in shortening with pastry
blender or however you like best. Mix thoroughly.
Stir in milk to make a soft dough and work lightly on
floured board. Roll or pat out to desired thickness.
Cut out with floured biscuit cutter. Brush with
melted butter (optional). Bake in a hot oven, 425°,
for about 12-15 minutes.

*We usually prick the unbaked biscuits with a fork to prevent
them from puffing. These biscuits keep quite well in the
freezer. Just make sure that you wrap them up tightly.*

*A good hearty vegetable soup with biscuits, a salad and dessert
make for fine eating.*

ESTHER PERKINS' BISCUITS

2 cups flour, sifted
4 teaspoons baking powder
½ teaspoon salt
½ cup vegetable shortening (lard or Crisco preferred)
¾ cup milk, enough to make a soft dough

Sift the flour, baking powder and salt together. Cut in the shortening until the pieces are the size of a pea. Gradually add the milk. Pat out dough until it is thick enough to cut with biscuit cutter. Place on greased cookie sheet. Bake at 450° for 12-15 minutes or until biscuits are brown.

Courtesy of Ruth Nutter.

HERB BISCUITS

4 cups flour
3 rounded teaspoons baking powder
3 tablespoons sugar
3 teaspoons of either Shaker Thyme, Dill, Basil, Chervil or Marjoram
1 teaspoon salt
6 tablespoons shortening
2 cups milk

Sift flour, baking powder, sugar and salt together. Mix in the herb. Cut in shortening until pieces are the size of a pea. Gradually add in the milk until it is all well mixed. Roll out on a lightly floured board to an inch thickness. Cut out and place on greased cookie sheets. Bake in a 425° oven for 20-30 minutes or until browned.

HERB-CHEESE ROLLS

½ cup very warm water
2 packages yeast
1½ cups warm water
1 tablespoon sugar
2 teaspoons salt
5 cups sifted flour
½ cup grated Parmesan cheese
½ cup Shaker Parsley
1 teaspoon Shaker Oregano
1 teaspoon Shaker Basil
1 egg white
1 tablespoon water

Pour very warm water into a large bowl. Sprinkle in yeast and stir until yeast is dissolved. Add the remaining water, sugar, salt and 2½ cups of the flour. Beat together until well mixed. Stir in the remaining flour and mix until smooth. Knead the dough on a lightly floured board. Knead for 5 minutes. Turn into a greased bowl, cover and let rise in a warm place until doubled in bulk, about 30 minutes. Meanwhile, combine the cheese with the parsley, oregano and basil. Punch down the dough and divide in half.

Roll one half on a floured board to make a 9 x 5-inch rectangle. Spread dough with melted butter and sprinkle with herb-cheese mixture. Roll up dough jelly roll style so that the roll is 15″ long. Cut into 1″ slices. Place in a greased muffin tins, seam side down. Repeat with the remaining dough. Cover and rise until double in bulk, about 30 minutes. Bake in a 400° oven for 15 minutes.

Remove from oven. Brush with egg white that has been beaten with the water. Return to oven and bake for 10 minutes longer. Cool on wire racks for crispiness. Yields 2½ dozen rolls.

FOUR HOUR ROLLS

1 package yeast
2 tablespoons sugar
¼ cup lukewarm water
2 eggs, beaten
¼ cup sugar
¾ cup water
¼ cup shortening, melted
1 teaspoon salt
4 cups flour

Dissolve yeast and sugar in the ¼ cup of water. Add remaining ingredients. Place in a greased bowl and cover away from drafts. Allow to rise for 2 hours in a warm place. Shape into rolls (should produce 18 rolls). No kneading is necessary. Let rise in greased baking tin for 30-35 minutes or until double in bulk. Bake at 425° for 15-20 minutes, depending on size.

SISTER MARIE'S DELICIOUS PANCAKES

1½ cups flour
2½ teaspoons baking powder
3 tablespoons sugar
1 egg, beaten
1 cup milk
3 tablespoons shortening
¾ teaspoons salt

Sift flour, baking powder, sugar and salt together. Combine egg, milk and shortening. Add to dry ingredients all at once, beating with a spoon until smooth. Fry in a pan that has been lightly greased.

We only grease the pan once. As later batches are made, we rub the surface with a raw carrot. This eliminates the need of extra grease and browns the pancakes perfectly. If you are making a large batch you will need to cut off a slice of carrot every so often to ensure its browning ability.

BROTHER TED'S WAFFLES

2 eggs
2 teaspoons sugar
2 cups milk
2 cups flour
3 teaspoons baking powder
½ cup butter, melted

Combine the eggs, sugar, milk, flour, and baking powder. Beat thoroughly and then stir in the melted butter.

CURRANT SCONES

2 cups all-purpose flour
1½ teaspoons cream of tartar
¾ teaspoon baking soda
1 teaspoon salt
½ cup butter or margarine
½ cup currants
1 egg
1 egg yolk, reserve for topping
¾ cup buttermilk
Sugar

Sift flour, cream of tartar, baking soda and salt into a bowl. Cut in butter. Add currants, whole egg and buttermilk. Mix well and turn out onto a well floured board. Knead a few times and then roll or pat out the dough to approximately ½" thickness. Cut into 2" diamonds. Place on cookie sheets and prick tops several times with fork. Beat egg yolk with a little cold water and brush on scones. Sprinkle with sugar. Bake in 425° oven for about 15 minutes. Makes about 2 dozen.

The scones are very good. Our family enjoys them tremendously. They go well with chowders.

BRAN MUFFINS

1 cup All-Bran
1 cup milk
1 egg
¼ cup oil
1½ cups sugar
3 teaspoons baking powder
½ teaspoon salt

Combine milk and All-Bran. Let stand about 2 minutes or until most of the moisture is absorbed. Add shortening and egg. Mix well. Sift together the flour, sugar, salt and baking powder. Add to the All-Bran mixture stirring only until combined. Fill greased muffin tins three quarters full. Bake in 400° oven about 24 minutes.

POPOVERS

2 cups flour
1 teaspoon salt
4 eggs
2 cups milk
2 tablespoons melted shortening

Sift flour; add salt and then sift again. Beat eggs until light and thick. Add flour and 1/3 cup milk until all the flour is moistened. Add remaining milk and

shortening. Beat well until the mixture is free of lumps. Fill the muffin tins less than half full. Bake at 425° for 40-50 minutes.

SISTER MILDRED'S DOUGHNUTS

1 cup sugar
2 tablespoons melted lard
1 egg, beaten
1 cup sour buttermilk
1 teaspoon baking soda
3 cups flour
2 teaspoons nutmeg
½ teaspoon ginger*
Pinch of salt

Cream the sugar, lard and egg together. Dissolve the soda in milk and add to the creamed mixture. Gradually add the flour, nutmeg, ginger and salt. Roll out on floured board to ¼" thickness. Cut out and fry in deep fat (375°).

The doughnuts originate from the time when Sister Mildred lived at the Alfred Community. They made many of these doughnuts for sale. With all due apology to Dunkin' Donuts and others, these doughnuts have some real substance to them. They are very good.

*Adding ginger to the dough cuts down on the amount of grease that the doughnuts take on during frying. There is no added taste of ginger in the final product.

SEAFOOD

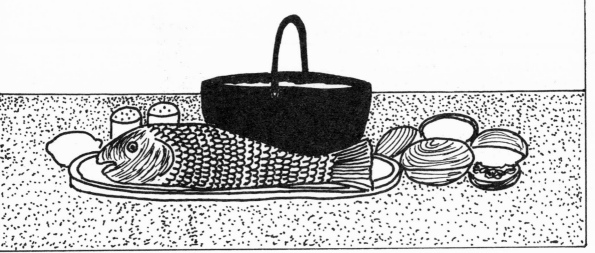

SHAKER FISH & EGG

2 cups rich milk or light cream
1 tablespoon butter or margarine
3 boiled potatoes, sliced thin (they are better
   if cold when used)
1 cup codfish, boiled and shredded
6 hard boiled eggs
¼ teaspoon salt
Dash of pepper
Scant ½ teaspoon Shaker Fines Herbes

Scald milk and add butter. In a buttered baking dish or casserole place a layer of boiled potatoes. Then place a layer of codfish and finally a layer of eggs. Repeat until the dish is filled, or you have what you want. Add seasonings. Cover with the hot milk. With a knife or spoon allow milk to seep down through the mixture. Cook in a slow oven at 325° for 50 minutes or until all the milk has been absorbed. Garnish top with Shaker Parsley. Serves 6.

This recipe has been used in every Shaker cookbook ever published. It is a favorite of the Shaker family here at Sabbathday Lake. About thirty years ago it used to be considered a rather economical dish, especially when we had our own dairy herd. The cream and butter were plentiful then, and a pound of salted codfish cost only 39¢. Today it is $2.98 and still it climbs.

I have fond memories of Eldress Prudence Stickney making this dish for our family when it numbered 60 people. She used huge double boilers. Even though she was at this time the spiritual leader of the community, she still enjoyed cooking and would often come into the kitchen to help the cooks. She was usually attired in a long, floor length dress with just the tops of her shoes showing. With her Shaker cap on she left a lasting and memorable picture. Eldress Prudence was a tiny person and often seemed dwarfed by the stove and large kettles.

SISTER FRANCES' SPECIAL BAKED FISH

Filet of frozen haddock or flounder
French dressing
Cracker crumbs
Melted butter

Thaw fish until just unfrozen. Immerse fish in French dressing. Then coat both sides with cracker crumbs. Place on a greased baking sheet. Pour melted butter over it and bake in a very hot oven, 425°-450°, for 10 minutes. Serve at once.

If you like cheese flavor, use cheese crackers, as it will give you a good flavor as well as rich color. Otherwise you should use saltines.

This is an excellent way to use frozen fish as it doesn't dry out as most frozen fish does.

SALT CODFISH

1 pound salt cod
1½ cups milk
3 tablespoons butter or margarine
3 tablespoons flour
Dash of Shaker Fines Herbes
1 hard boiled egg, chopped

Pre-soak the fish overnight in cold water. When ready to use, drain fish and cut into bite size pieces. Simmer gently for 15 minutes. Melt butter over low heat. Thoroughly mix flour into butter and slowly add milk, stirring constantly until smooth. Add seasonings and cook over low heat for a few minutes. Add fish to sauce and serve over toast or boiled potatoes. Garnish with hard boiled egg.

CODFISH CAKES

1 pound codfish
2 cups cold potatoes, boiled or mashed
2 eggs, beaten
2 medium onions, minced

Soak the codfish overnight. When ready to use, slowly boil for 10-15 minutes. Shred fish. Add potatoes, eggs and onions. Mix thoroughly. Form into cakes with hands. It may be necessary to flour your hands to keep the mixture from sticking to your hands. Pan fry in oil over moderate heat until patties are browned on both sides.

This is excellent served with baked beans or as a main dish with vegetables.

OYSTER STEW

2 pints oysters
Dash of pepper
2 tablespoons crackers (I use saltines rolled fine)
4 cups rich milk (You may substitute a can of evaporated milk and 3 cups of milk)
4 tablespoons butter or margarine
¼ teaspoon Shaker Fines Herbes

Cook the oysters in their liquid (over a low heat) until sides begin to curl. Heat the milk and melt the butter in it. Add to the oysters. Add cracker crumbs and cook over a low heat until the milk thickens slightly. Taste for salt, as the cracker crumbs will add salt. Add Shaker Fines Herbes and heat until very hot, but don't allow to boil. Serve with a sprig of parsley.

We would often have this oyster stew for Easter dinner. Eldress Prudence Stickney would cook it in the large arch kettle which is still in use in the Community's kitchen. As it was made with the good butter and cream from our own dairy, it was a real gourmet's delight. Today, because of the increase in the price of oysters, it has become a rare treat.

SALMON MOUSSE

3 tablespoons lemon juice
¼ cup chopped onion
1 envelope gelatin
½ cup boiling water
½ cup mayonnaise
2 teaspoons paprika
2 teaspoons Shaker Dill
1-lb. can salmon, drained
1 cup whipping cream

In a blender add the lemon juice, onion, gelatin and boiling water. Mix on high for a minute or so. Then add the remaining ingredients except for the cream. Blend on high speed for another minute. Finally add in the cream and blend for a minute. Lightly grease a mold and pour salmon into mold. Refrigerate for 3 or 4 hours.

TUNA-TYHME LOAF

3 7-ounce cans tuna fish, drained and flaked
1½ cups soft bread crumbs
½ cup milk
2 eggs, beaten
2 tablespoons chopped onion
1 teaspoon salt
½ teaspoon garlic powder

1 teaspoon Shaker Parsley
1 teaspoon Shaker Thyme
¼ teaspoon pepper
Juice of ½ lemon

Mix all the ingredients together thoroughly in the order given. Pack into a 1½ quart buttered loaf pan. Bake uncovered in a preheated 375° oven for 1 hour or until browned on the top. Serve with egg sauce.

BASIC WHITE SAUCE

For medium sauce:

2 tablespoons butter or margarine
2 tablespoons flour
¼ teaspoon salt
Dash of pepper
¼ teaspoon Shaker Fines Herbes
1 cup milk

Melt the butter over low heat. Blend in the flour and seasonings, mixing very thoroughly. Slowly add milk, mixing well as you combine. Cook rapidly, stirring constantly until sauce thickens. Cook approximately 2 minutes longer. Yields approximately 1 cup.

For thick sauce:

Use 4 tablespoons of butter and 4 tablespoons of flour. Follow the same procedure as for the medium sauce.

For thin sauce:

Use 1 tablespoon butter and 1 tablespoon flour. Follow the same procedure as for the medium sauce.

Egg Sauce:

Add 2 hard cooked eggs, chopped, to the basic white sauce.

SALMON LOAF

1 large can red salmon
3 eggs, separated
½ teaspoon salt
¼ teaspoon pepper
½ teaspoon Shaker Fines Herbes
¼ cup melted butter or margarine
3 tablespoons lemon juice
1½ cups firmly packed soft bread crumbs
1½ cups scalded milk

Remove all bones and skin from the salmon and flake. Beat egg yolks and add salt, pepper, fines herbes, butter, lemon juice and bread crumbs. Mix thoroughly. Add milk and mix well. Beat egg whites until stiff. Fold into salmon mixture. Bake in a greased loaf pan at 375° for 1 hour.

This may be served with a thin white sauce and garnished with sliced hard boiled eggs, or may be served plain with a garnish of parsley.

RICE & TUNA MOLD

3 cups cold cooked rice
1½ cups celery, finely chopped
1 7-ounce can tuna, drained and flaked
1/3 cup chopped pickle
2 tablespoons Shaker Parsley
½ cup mayonnaise
½ cup sour cream
1 tablespoon lemon juice
Dash of salt and pepper to taste
1/3 cup diced pimento

Combine the first 5 ingredients together. Then combine the mayonnaise, sour cream, lemon juice, seasonings and pimento together. Combine the 2 mixtures together and blend thoroughly. Pack into a 1-quart mold. Chill for at least 1 hour. Unmold and garnish with sliced hard cooked eggs, tomatoes, olives, or whatever suits you. Serves 6.

This makes a good summer meal when served with rolls or potato chips.

MAINE FISH CHOWDER

¼ pound salt pork, diced
3 onions, sliced
4 cups raw potato, cut up, sliced or diced
2 2¼-lbs. fish filet (With the price of fish, I have found that the frozen is as good as the fresh, although I prefer fresh.)
1 teaspoon salt
¼ teaspoon pepper
1 quart rich milk (if you do not have rich milk evaporated will do)
1 tablespoon butter
1 teaspoon Shaker Fines Herbes

Fry salt pork over a low heat until it is crisp and brown. Drain off most of the grease. Add onion and pork pieces to potato. Cook in just enough water to keep the mixture from sticking or catching on. Cut fish into large pieces. When the potato is almost done add fish. Cook with potato until it is tender and falls apart easily. Add the seasonings, milk and butter. Heat just to the boiling point.

The Shaker Fines Herbes gives the chowder a different and delicious flavor.

CLAM CHOWDER

¼ pound salt pork, cut up fine
1 quart potatoes, cut up into small chunks
2 large onions, chopped
1 quart clams or more, drained, but reserve juice
2 quarts rich milk

Fry the pork in a frying pan until brown and crisp. Be careful not to burn. Drain off most of the fat from the pork. Add the pork to a large kettle. Add potatoes and onions with just enough water so it will not stick. The less water used the better. Cook over low heat until done. Add the clams to the potato and onion mixture. Bring to a boil. Let cook for 2 or 3 minutes, as the longer they cook, the tougher the clams become. When you add the clams add the juice as well. Add the hot milk. Make sure that the chowder doesn't boil after the milk has been added. Just about a half hour before serving, season with salt and, if you like, 1 teaspoon Shaker Fines Herbes. Serve very hot. Add a piece of butter just before serving.

It has been many years since we have been able to afford fresh clams, but we think our chowder is as good as any fresh clam chowder, even though we use canned clams. In using canned clams drain the liquid off and use this liquid instead of water to cook the potatoes and onions in. When potatoes are almost but not quite done, add canned clams and allow to cook for a short time. Add the seasonings as for fresh clams. We like our chowder fairly thin and then add a cracker to it. For a thicker chowder, add about ½ cup cracker crumbs 20 minutes before serving.

This was a great treat at our bi-centennial conference, using canned clams. We found that a piece of butter put on just before serving adds much flavor.

CLAM FRITTERS

1 pint chopped canned clams, drained, but
   reserve juice
2 cups cracker crumbs
2 eggs
¼ teaspoon Shaker Fines Herbes

Mix clams and crumbs together. Add eggs one at a time and mix well. Refrigerate for 1 hour before frying. Fry in butter or margarine. Drop large tablespoons into the hot butter. Fry on one side until brown, then turn and brown the other side. If using saltine crackers do not add salt, otherwise salt may be added. If the mixture seems stiff, add in some of the liquid from the clams.

This is a very good and easy recipe. We have found that Colby students love them!

CLAM SOUFFLE

4 eggs, separated
½ cup milk
2 cups soft bread crumbs
1 tablespoon butter or margarine
2 cans' minced clams, drained, but reserve the juice
1 cup clam juice (If not enough juice for 1 cup,
   add extra milk to make the 1 cup of liquid.)
1 teaspoon Shaker Fines Herbes

Beat egg yolks and let stand for 10 minutes. Add milk, clam juice, bread crumbs, butter, minced clams and Shaker Fines Herbes. Beat the egg whites until stiff. Fold whites into the clam mixture. Bake in a greased casserole at 350° for 35-40 minutes.

SISTER FRANCES' MUSSELS

10 pounds mussels, well scrubbed
White wine
1 large onion, chopped fine
1 teaspoon Shaker Fines Herbes
1 clove garlic, chopped fine

The most important step in preparing mussels is to scrub them. This must be done until you have removed all doubt of any sand being present. After scrubbing the mussels, place them in a large kettle with about ½" of white wine. Add the onion, fines herbes and garlic. Cover kettle and let steam until the shells have opened. Serves 5.

Mussels are a good and inexpensive dish right now, so I came up with this little recipe for them.

Every time we have had them we have unexpected company, so we have not had any left over. Thus we have yet to prepare a chowder from the mussel leftovers.

GRILLED FISH

¼ cup butter or margarine
¼ cup Shaker Tarragon Vinegar
1 tablespoon lemon juice
1 clove garlic, crushed
½ teaspoon Shaker Tarragon
½ teaspoon salt
1½-2 pounds whole fish: bass, flounder or trout

In a small saucepan combine butter, Tarragon Vinegar, garlic, tarragon and salt. Clean fish and score. Adjust the grill to 5" from the prepared coals. Place fish on a well oiled strip of foil. Grill 12 to 15 minutes per pound. Turn once and brush frequently with the sauce.

BROILED SCALLOPS

1 pound sea scallops
1 tablespoon Shaker Tarragon Vinegar
¼ cup butter or margarine, melted
Salt & pepper
Paprika

Rinse the scallops, drain and dry them with paper towels. Arrange scallops on broiler rack. Combine the butter and Tarragon Vinegar. Brush half of the mixture over scallops. Sprinkle with salt, pepper and paprika. Broil, 5 inches from the heat, for 3 minutes. Turn scallops and brush with the remaining mixture. Sprinkle salt, pepper and paprika again. Broil 2 or 3 minutes longer, or until scallops are tender.

POULTRY

CHICKEN TARRAGON

1 2½-lb. frying chicken
Salt
Shaker Tarragon

Thoroughly wash and wipe dry with paper towels a fryer-size chicken. Rub salt over the cavity and over the outside of the chicken. If you are on a salt-free diet, a salt substitute may be used with good results. After salting, rub tarragon over the chicken in the same manner as the salt. Bake for approximately 2 hours, depending on size, in a 300° oven. When serving either cut into quarters or halves, depending on the appetite of those eating it.

The tarragon gives the chicken a wonderful flavor.

SISTER FRANCES' BREAD STUFFING

2 pounds white bread, broken into small pieces
2 cups hot water
1 cup butter or margarine, melted
2 cups chopped onion
2 eggs, beaten lightly
2 tablespoons Shaker Sage, crushed
Salt and pepper to taste

Pour water and melted butter over bread. Allow bread to soften. Saute onions over low heat until just tender, do not overcook. Add eggs, onions and seasonings to bread. Mix thoroughly. Taste, or better still have others around you taste, as it makes it interesting to add whatever bit of seasonings others may like. In addition to the sage, I like to add approximately 1 teaspoon of Bell's Seasoning.

Thoroughly wash the bird. Dry interior with paper towel. Thoroughly rub interior with mixture of butter and sage. Rub all over bird, giving special heed to wing areas. Roast at 300° for the recommended time for the bird.

Because we eat very little white bread, we use whole wheat almost exclusively. I usually have a bag in the refrigerator in which I save all the odds and ends of white rolls, sandwich bread and toast from white breads. A few days before I intend to stuff a turkey or chicken, Sister Marie makes white bread which we keep in the refrigerator.

STUFFING #2

3 tablespoons butter or margarine
2 medium onions, minced
3 cups dried bread crumbs
3 tablespoons Shaker Celery Leaves
1 tablespoon Shaker Summer Savory

1 tablespoon Shaker Basil
1 tablespoon Shaker Thyme
1 teaspoon salt
¼ teaspoon pepper
½ cup hot water
3 tablespoons butter or margarine, melted

Melt butter and saute the onion until tender, but do not brown. Add onion to bread crumbs. Gradually add in the hot water and melted butter. Mix well.

CHICKEN A LA KING

¼ cup butter or margarine, melted
½ green pepper, chopped
2 tablespoons minced onion
2 tablespoons chopped pimento
¼ cup mushrooms (fresh are superior, but
   I often use canned with good results)
3 tablespoons flour
½ teaspoon salt
1 cup chicken broth
½ cup milk
½ cup heavy cream (you may substitute
   evaporated milk)
2 egg yolks, slightly beaten
2 cups cooked chicken, cubed

In hot butter saute the pepper, onion and mushrooms until tender. Do not overcook. Usually 5 minutes of cooking is sufficient. Remove from heat and slowly stir in flour until smooth. Blend in chicken broth and milk. Cook over low heat stirring constantly until mixture thickens and begins to boil. Blend cream into slightly beaten egg yolks and add to sauce. Add chicken and gently reheat. This may be served on rice, toast or biscuits. We prefer to use herb biscuits.

CHICKEN STEW

5-lb. ready-to-cook stewing chicken,
   cut into serving pieces
¼ cup butter or margarine
1 small onion, sliced
2 celery stalks, sliced
1 carrot, sliced
2 tablespoons Shaker Tarragon Vinegar
1 teaspoon Shaker Fines Herbes
1 bay leaf
Salt and pepper
Boiling water

In hot butter in a large kettle, brown the chicken pieces on both sides. Remove from heat. Add the onion, celery, carrot, Tarragon Vinegar, Shaker Fines Herbes, bay leaf, salt and pepper. Add boiling water to cover. Bring to boiling, reduce heat and allow to simmer covered for 2 hours or until chicken is tender. Delicious with hot herb biscuits.

SWEDISH STYLE CHICKEN

2 3-lb. frying chickens
Salt and pepper to taste
2 medium onions, sliced
Olive or vegetable oil for frying
1 cup water

Cut the fryers into convenient serving pieces. Salt and pepper well. Heat enough olive oil in a large skillet to fry the chicken. The oil should be very hot. Place the chicken pieces in the hot oil, being careful not to crowd the pan. Brown well on both sides, turning with a wooden spoon or fork. When golden brown transfer the pieces to an enameled cooking vessel. Intermix the sliced onion with the chicken pieces. Add the water and simmer for approximately 1 hour or until the chicken is fork tender. The chicken may be served as is or with the following gravy.

SOUR CREAM MUSHROOM GRAVY

2 tablespoons fat from frying chicken
2 tablespoons butter or margarine
4 tablespoons flour
1 cup milk
1 cup sour cream
1 cup lightly sauteed fresh mushrooms

Salt and pepper to taste
¼ teaspoon paprika

When the chicken has been fried, reserve the 2 tablespoons of fat from the pan. Add the butter. Heat and stir in the flour. Cook, stirring constantly for approximately 2 to 3 minutes. Add the milk and sour cream as well as salt and pepper (freshly ground is best) to taste. Cook over a low heat for approximately 4-5 minutes, stirring constantly. Add the sauteed mushrooms and paprika just before serving.

Brother Ted has often made this recipe and wrapped the serving dish (the same dish in which it was cooked) in newspapers to take for a picnic. It is wonderful. It is just cool enough to easily eat at an out-of-doors table.

ORIENTAL MARINADE

For a 2-lb. chicken:

3 tablespoons soy sauce
2 tablespoons sherry
2-3 slices fresh ginger or preserved stem ginger
1 clove garlic, crushed
1 teaspoon honey
1 teaspoon salt

Marinate the chicken for an hour, then place it in the oven with the marinade on it and bake 1¾-2 hours at 350°.

CHICKEN AND RICE ROSEMARY

2 cups diced chicken
½ cup regular uncooked rice
1 cup sliced mushrooms
1/3 cup slivered almonds
¼ teaspoon Shaker Rosemary
¼ teaspoon Shaker Thyme
½ teaspoon salt
2½ cups chicken broth

Place all of the above ingredients in a buttered casserole dish. Stir together carefully so as not to break up the chicken cubes. Bake in a 350° oven uncovered for 50 minutes or until rice is tender and the top is browned. Do not stir during baking.

If used as a main course I usually serve a cream sauce with it to add body and moisture. It is good as is if served with salad or side dish.

CHICKEN OR TURKEY PIE

2 cups chicken or turkey, cut into cubes or
  chunky pieces
2 cups gravy
2 tablespoons minced onion
½ teaspoon Shaker Fines Herbes
Pastry for one 9″ crust

Combine the ingredients together. Pour into a glass pie plate or individual ramekins. Cover with pastry and bake at 450° for 15 minutes. Reduce heat to 350° and continue baking until crust is browned and gravy has begun to bubble through.

SISTER FRANCES' CHICKEN CACCIATORE

2 tablespoons butter or margarine
2 tablespoons olive oil
2 broiler fryers, approximately 2½ lbs.,
  cut up
2 garlic cloves, minced
1 cup chopped onion
1 teaspoon salt

¼ teaspoon pepper
½ teaspoon Shaker Rosemary
1 tablespoon Shaker Parsley
1 28-ounce can tomatoes

Heat butter with oil in large skillet. Brown chicken pieces well on all sides. Cook only a few pieces at one time. Remove from skillet and drain off oil. Reserve approximately 1 tablespoon. Saute garlic and onion together until tender. Add seasonings, herbs and tomatoes. Break up tomatoes into large pieces. Return the chicken to skillet, cover and simmer for 45 minutes or until chicken is tender. Remove chicken to serving platter. Allow sauce to simmer for a few minutes until it thickens. Pour over chicken. Garnish with fresh parsley. Serves 6.

This is a good meal when served with rice pilaf and salad.

MEATS

CORNED BEEF HASH

4 boiled potatoes, peeled prior to boiling
1 12-ounce can corned beef
½ onion, chopped
1 teaspoon salt (optional)
Dash of pepper to taste
¼ cup butter or margarine

Chop the potatoes and meat together. Do not use a grinder. I usually chop the pieces rather finely although it all comes together well. Add the onion, seasonings and mix well. Heat the butter slowly in a large skillet. Turn the hash mixture into a skillet, pressing down firmly with a spatula. Cook over medium heat for 15 minutes. A light brown crust will form on the bottom. Turn frequently. Just before serving, allow the crust to form without breaking. Turn hash out onto a platter. Top with poached eggs and a bit of Shaker Parsley.

This is a great favorite here. Usually we have it once every 2 weeks. Be sure to have plenty of ketchup on hand.

HAMBURG PIE

1 pound ground beef
½ cup chopped onion

2 cups cooked green beans (canned may be used with good results), drained
2 cans tomato soup, undiluted
Mashed potato topper*

In a skillet combine the meat, onion and a dash of salt and pepper. Brown the meat lightly. Add the drained beans and soup. Pour into a 1½ quart casserole. Drop potato topper over the casserole in mounds. Bake at 350° for 25-30 minutes.

*POTATO TOPPER

5 medium potatoes, cooked
½ cup warm milk
1 egg, beaten
Salt and pepper

Mash the cooked potatoes. While hot add the warm milk and beaten egg. Season to taste.

Sister Elizabeth always made this recipe. It is really good and we always look forward to having it.

BROTHER TED'S SWEDISH MEAT BALLS

1½ pounds hamburg (good and lean with very little fat) or preferably
1 pound hamburg with ½ pound of ground pork
½ cup bread crumbs
2 eggs, slightly beaten
2 cups light cream (I often substitute evaporated milk if I do not have cream)
1 teaspoon salt
¼ teaspoon pepper
¼ teaspoon Shaker Bouquet Garni
¼ teaspoon nutmeg
½ tablespoon molasses

Combine all of the above ingredients using only half of the cream and blend well. Form into small balls and place on greased cookie sheet. Bake for 20 minutes in a 350° oven or until browned. Remove and keep the meat balls warm while you prepare the sauce as follows:

Measure 2 tablespoons of fat from baking pan into a saucepan. Stir in 2 tablespoons flour and 1 package of instant beef broth. Cook, stirring constantly until just bubbly. Stir in the remaining cream and continue cooking until the sauce thickens and bubbles for about 1 minute. Add the meat balls and simmer over low heat until thoroughly heated. Serve over noodles on a heated platter. Garnish lightly with Shaker Bouquet Garni.

If time is of essence and you need to feed a larger amount of people, this may be doubled easily. Also for a quick sauce simmer the meat balls in 1 can of beef broth. Add 1 can of cream of mushroom soup and 1 pint of sour cream. Keep hot but do not allow to boil.

This is a favorite at the Community and it is always a part of the Christmas Eve smorgasbord.

Makes 6 servings. If you want a different hors d'oeuvre make tiny meat balls and serve them on tooth picks. Prepare a dish of sauce for your guests to dip from.

SWISS STEAK

1½ pounds round steak, or any inexpensive boneless steak, cut about 1″ thick (thinner steak will not tolerate the pounding)
¼ cup all-purpose flour
Salt and pepper to taste
3 tablespoons vegetable oil
1 large onion, sliced
½ cup sliced celery
1 8-ounce can stewed tomatoes
¼ teaspoon each of Shaker Basil, Shaker Oregano, and Shaker Thyme

With a meat mallet (or, if you do not have one, use the edge of a heavy saucer) pound the flour into both sides of the meat. Be sure to use all the flour if possible, as it makes the gravy while the meat cooks. Sprinkle the meat with salt and pepper. In a large skillet, (We have two wonderful Dutch ovens made of cast iron that were brought over from Alfred in 1931. They are perfect for this type of cooking.), heat oil and brown meat over medium high heat on all sides. Add the onion and celery which have been lightly cooked. Stir in the tomatoes and herbs. Be sure that the steak is covered with the tomatoes. Cover the dish tightly. If you do not have a covered dish, use foil wrapped tightly over the dish. Bake in a 300° oven until the meat is tender, usually 1½ hours. Use your judgment.

This is excellent served with noodles or rice and a green salad.

IRISH STEW

3 pounds pre-cooked lamb
3 slices salt pork
12 small white onions
6 large potatoes, cut into cubes
¼ cup Shaker Parsley
½ cup flour
1 teaspoon salt
½ teaspoon Shaker Thyme
Pepper to taste

Place one half of the meat in the stewing pot. Top with a layer consisting of half the salt pork, onions, potatoes and parsley. Repeat with the remaining meat and vegetables.

Combine the flour, thyme, salt and pepper with 4 cups of water. Pour over the meat and vegetables. Bring to a boil, reduce heat, cover and *simmer* for 1½ hours. Stir well, cover again and cook for 30 minutes. Serves 6.

HAMBURG CASSEROLE

1½ cups diced potato
1 cup diced carrots
1 can peas, drained, but reserve the juice
2 medium onions, diced
1 pound hamburg, more if desired
1 tablespoon flour
½ teaspoon Shaker Thyme

Cook the potatoes and carrots in the juice drained from the peas. Add extra water if necessary. Fry the onions and hamburg until lightly browned. Thicken the liquid, from the cooked vegetables, with the flour. Add to the hamburg mixture. Add the Shaker Thyme to mixture. Line a buttered casserole dish with a layer of potatoes and carrots, then a layer of peas on top of that. Finally a layer of hamburg and onions. Bake in a 350° oven for 30 minutes.

ROAST LEG OF VEAL

1 4-5 pound boneless leg of veal
1 medium onion, coarsely sliced
1 teaspoon salt (*optional*)
¼ teaspoon pepper
1 teaspoon crushed Shaker Rosemary
2 tablespoons butter or margarine

Wipe the roast with damp paper towels. Thoroughly mix the seasonings into a paste made of the softened butter. Before applying the paste to the roast, cut several small slits into the fat side of the roast. Place pieces of onion into the slits. With hands rub the seasoned butter paste thoroughly all over the roast. Place fat side up on rack in shallow roasting pan. Roast the veal, uncovered, in a slow oven (300°), allowing about 35 minutes per pound. If you use a meat thermometer it should register between 165° and 170° when the veal is cooked.

Veal was prepared in Shaker kitchens long before it became popular in haute cuisine restaurants. I have vivid memories from childhood of the veal being brought from the butchering and hung to ripen. Sister Ethel, God bless her, would love to call the children and young people together to see the heart and tongue of the young cow. She would tell us, "Now there is a tongue that never told a lie nor said an unkind word." The heart and tongue would often be combined in a cream sauce and served on toast. Although as young people we were all turned off by the dish, I now realize that it was quite a gourmet treat.

BROTHER ARNOLD'S VEAL SCHNITZEL

1½ pounds thin veal cutlets
¼ cup flour
4 tablespoons grated Parmesan cheese
1 egg, beaten
1 teaspoon Shaker Parsley
½ teaspoon salt (*optional*)
¼ teaspoon Shaker Rosemary
¾ cup milk
½ cup butter or margarine

Thoroughly combine flour, cheese, egg, herbs, salt and milk. Beat until smooth. Dip the cutlets into this mixture. Melt the butter in heavy frying pan. Add cutlets and fry over low heat for 3 to 4 minutes on each side until golden brown. Do not overcook or undercook. Remove to a hot platter and add just enough hot water to pan juices to make enough pan gravy to pour over cutlets. Garnish with sprigs of fresh parsley.

Although I, personally, do not approve of the method used in raising tender white veal (feeding creatures on skimmed milk), it has become a very popular dish and is one of the Brother's favorites. In Brother Delmer's day he did not concentrate on raising the white veal, so most of our veal dishes were either roasts or stews.

BROTHER ARNOLD'S LASAGNA WITH MEAT SAUCE

1-pound box lasagna
1 medium onion, chopped
1 garlic clove, minced
¼ cup oil (olive oil is best)
½ pound hamburg
2 pounds canned tomatoes, chopped
1 6-ounce can tomato paste
2 teaspoons Shaker Basil
2 teaspoons Shaker Oregano
1 teaspoon salt
¼ teaspoon pepper
1 pound Ricotta cheese
1 pound Mozzarella cheese sliced
1 8-ounce jar of grated Parmesan cheese

Brown the beef in a large skillet. Drain off the grease. In a large kettle saute the onions and garlic in oil until soft. Add the drained hamburg and simmer for 2 or 3 minutes. Add the tomatoes, tomato paste and all of the seasonings. Simmer uncovered for an hour or more. Stir occasionally to prevent sticking.

While the sauce is simmering cook the lasagna according to the directions on the package. Drain.

To assemble, spoon a little of the sauce on the bottom of a 13″ x 9″ pan. Arrange lasagna pieces over the sauce. Spoon the ricotta, mozzarella and Parmesan cheeses over the lasagna. Then spoon the sauce over the cheese. Repeat this process until the pan is filled or you run out of ingredients. Top with mozzarella. Bake in a 350° oven for 50-60 minutes.

LAZY DAY STEW

2 pounds beef cubes
Carrots
Potatoes
Onions
1 cup water
1 teaspoon sugar
Salt and pepper
2 teaspoons instant tapioca

Arrange the beef cubes in a single layer in a baking dish. There is no need to brown the meat first. Add chunks of carrots, potatoes and onions to suit. Add the sugar to the water and pour over the mixture. Add salt and pepper to taste. Sprinkle tapioca over the top of the meat mixture. Seal the pan with foil. Bake in a 350° oven for 3 hours.

Your dinner is ready in one dish. It is best served with a green salad.

Although we have had sheep here for many years, and we number at this time a flock of seventy, we never raised them with the intention of using them for food. Our thought was for the wool which we turned into yarn. The yarn is both for our own use and for sale. It is also used for the workshops which are given here at the Community.

When we had only a few sheep we named them all. There were, for example, Pyramus, Thisbe, Persephone, Clytemnestra and Demeter. It was for us impossible to think of serving up a lamb that we had petted and known by name. However, as the flock increased and the price of food along with it, we put our Yankee practicality to good use and began to have lamb more often on the table. As the cook I find it easier all around not to become involved with the lambs any longer, other than to prepare a dish for the table. One of our favorites is the following leg of lamb.

LEG OF LAMB

1 leg of lamb, 5-6 pounds
1 clove of garlic, minced
½ cup salad oil
2 cups dry red wine (I have found Burgundy to
    be superior)
3 onions, sliced
½ teaspoon cloves
2 teaspoons Shaker Oregano
2 teaspoons salt
Shaker Parsley for garnish

Wipe the lamb with damp paper towels. With a paring knife cut several slits in the fleshy part of the lamb and insert the slivers of garlic. If you are fond of garlic more may be added. Combine the remaining ingredients in a large shallow glass baking dish. I use our lovely old earthenware bowls which have been in the community for many years. Be sure that the lamb is as flat as possible in the dish. Pour marinade over the lamb. Refrigerate covered at least 24 hours, but baste and turn the lamb frequently. Preheat the oven to 325°. Place the lamb fat side up on a rack in roasting pan. Roast uncovered and baste occasionally for approximately 2½ hours. If you use a meat thermometer, cook until it registers 175° for medium. Allow the roast to rest for about 20 minutes before slicing.

The remaining marinade may be bottled and kept refrigerated for the next time that you serve leg of lamb.

LAMB BURGERS
(Baa Baa Burgers)

2 pounds ground lamb
2 garlic cloves, crushed
1 medium onion, finely chopped
¼ cup parsley
¼ cup dry bread crumbs
2 eggs
1 teaspoon salt
1 teaspoon pepper

1 teaspoon Shaker Oregano
1 teaspoon Shaker Thyme

Mix all ingredients together in a bowl. You may make them out into burgers or into meat balls or into a loaf.

CHEESEBURGER PIE

1 pound ground beef
½ cup evaporated milk
½ cup ketchup
1/3 cup fine dry bread crumbs
¾ teaspoon salt
¼ cup chopped onion
½ teaspoon Shaker Oregano
⅛ teaspoon pepper
1 8″ unbaked pastry shell
4 ounces processed American cheese, shredded
1 teaspoon Worcestershire sauce

Combine beef, milk, ketchup, bread crumbs, onion, salt, pepper and oregano. Mix thoroughly. Spread in the unbaked pastry shell. Bake in 350° oven for 35-40 minutes. Toss together cheese and Worcestershire sauce; spread atop the meat. Bake 10 minutes more. Remove from oven and let stand for 10 minutes before serving. Garnish with dill pickle slices if desired.

MEAT BALLS

1 pound hamburg
½ cup bread crumbs
1 egg
½ small onion, minced
1 clove garlic, crushed
1 teaspoon each of Shaker Basil, Shaker Oregano, and Shaker Thyme
1 teaspoon salt
½ teaspoon pepper
¼ cup Parmesan cheese

Mix the ingredients together in a bowl. Make sure that you mix them thoroughly. Shape into balls and brown them in a frying pan.

BEEF STROGANOFF

1½ pounds sirloin steak (at least 1″ thick)
2 cups raw mushrooms, sliced
2 medium onions, chopped fine
½ cup butter
¾ cup sour cream
1 teaspoon paprika
2 tablespoons soy sauce
2 tablespoons sherry
Pinch of nutmeg
Salt and pepper

Trim the sirloin removing the fat and cut the meat into 2″ strips going with the grain. Next slice the strips as thin as possible against the grain. In a frying pan melt the butter and add the paprika, onions and mushrooms. Saute until the onions are soft. Add the remaining ingredients, saving the sour cream. Stir-fry until the meat is cooked. This should take no longer than 2 minutes, so please do not overcook it. Add the sour cream and stir until hot. Serve immediately.

POT ROAST

1 pot roast, 4-5 pounds
1/3 cup flour
2 tablespoons fat
2 teaspoons salt
Dash of pepper
¼ teaspoon Shaker Celery Leaves
¼ teaspoon Shaker Oregano
3 tablespoons wine vinegar
1 medium onion, sliced
2 cups whole pearl onions
8 small carrots, pared (if they are really thick, slice once)
3 tablespoons flour
½ cup water

On waxed paper roll beef in flour to coat all sides. Heat the fat in a Dutch oven over medium heat and brown meat on all sides, turning as it browns. Sprinkle with salt and pepper as you brown the meat.

If the meat is of dubious quality, meat tenderizer may be liberally sprinkled on as it browns. It takes about 15 minutes to brown the meat. Add celery leaves, oregano, vinegar and the sliced onion. Cover tightly. Allow to simmer over low heat. Turn occasionally. Allow to cook approximately 3½ hours. Add the pearl onions and carrots. Cover and simmer another hour or until the meat is tender and the vegetables are done.

To make the gravy, skim off the fat from broth in Dutch oven. Add enough water to remaining broth to make 2½ cups of liquid. In a small bowl combine the flour with the water. Stir into the liquid and cook until thickened. To the gravy add a pinch of Shaker Thyme and a pinch of Shaker Basil.

MEAT LOAF

2 eggs
¼ cup milk
1 teaspoon salt (optional)
1 teaspoon Shaker Thyme
¼ teaspoon nutmeg (optional)
Dash of pepper
1½ cups soft bread crumbs (I prefer bread broken up to commercial bread crumbs)
2 pounds hamburg, as little fat as possible
2 tablespoons Shaker Parsley
¼ cup finely chopped onion

Preheat the oven to 350°. In a large bowl beat the eggs with the milk and seasonings. Add bread crumbs. Allow to stand 5 minutes. Add the meat, parsley and onions. Mix well until thoroughly combined. Grease a loaf pan and pack the meat loaf mixture lightly but firmly into the pan. Bake for one hour.

MEAT LOAF, SECOND CHOICE

1 can tomato soup (do not dilute - use it as it comes from the can)
2 pounds ground beef
1½ cups bread crumbs
½ cup finely chopped onion
1 egg, slightly beaten
2 tablespoons Shaker Parsley
½ teaspoon Shaker Basil
Dash of salt *(optional)*
Dash of pepper

Combine all ingredients and mix very thoroughly. Shape into a loaf and place in a shallow pan or place mixture in a loaf pan (this is what I use). Bake at 350° for 1 hour. If the loaf seems underdone continue to bake another 15 minutes. Serve with tomato sauce or mushroom gravy.

HERBED ROAST PORK

1 loin of pork, 3-4 pounds
2 tablespoons finely chopped onion
1 teaspoon salt *(optional)*
1 teaspoon Shaker Sage
½ teaspoon Shaker Thyme
¼ teaspoon Shaker Oregano
2 tablespoons butter or margarine, softened to make a paste

Wipe the roast with damp paper towels. Thoroughly mix the herbs and salt into the softened butter. With your hands spread the butter mixture over the entire roast, rubbing especially well into the meat portions. Place roast with fat side up into a shallow roasting pan. Sprinkle the onion over the top and around into the sides of the pan so that the juices coming from the roast will mingle with the onion. Roast for 3 hours or if you use a meat thermometer, which I do not, roast until thermometer registers at 185°.

We do not usually make gravy, but prefer to pour the fat off into the roasting pan, and when very hot add a bit of hot water for a browned broth. If you prefer a gravy, mix 2 tablespoons flour with the fat and add water. Stir constantly until thickened and season to desired taste.

Although we do eat roast pork and also enjoy pork chops now and then, we seem to have been influenced by Brother Delmer's feelings and we do not often have this meat.

A roast pork served with unsweetened apple sauce to which a few cinnamon candies have been added is a real feast. Roast pork is also good when served with red cabbage.

MARINARA SAUCE

1 clove garlic, minced
½ cup chopped onion
¼ cup olive oil
4 cups canned tomatoes
½ teaspoon Shaker Oregano
½ cup Shaker Parsley
2 tablespoons Shaker Basil Vinegar
Salt & pepper

Heat olive oil in medium-size skillet. Cook the garlic and onion until golden brown. Put the tomatoes through a food mill and add to the garlic-onion mixture. Add in the remaining ingredients and simmer, until thickened, approximately 1 hour.

This may be served with your favorite pasta dish, chicken, lamb, pork or fish too.

CASSEROLES

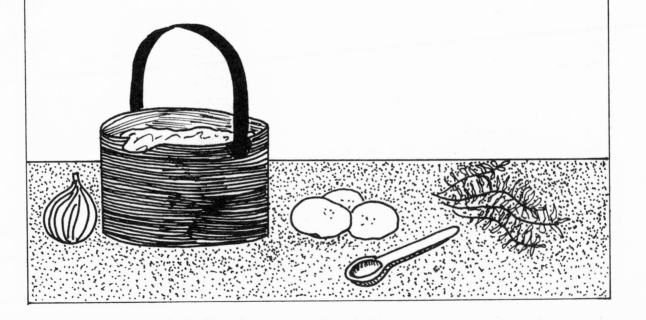

HAM 'N' NOODLE CASSEROLE

1½ cups cooked noodles
2 tablespoons butter or margarine
2 tablespoons flour
1 cup milk
1 cup grated cheese
2 tablespoons ketchup
½ teaspoon Shaker Fines Herbes
2 cups cooked ham, cut up
1 cup peas, drained
Bread crumbs
Melted butter

In a skillet, melt the butter and add flour. Stir until smooth. Gradually add milk and cook until thickened. Add the cheese and blend well. Add all the other ingredients stirring them until well mixed. Turn mixture into a baking dish. Top with buttered bread crumbs. Bake at 350° for 30 minutes.

EGGPLANT CASSEROLE

3 tablespoons butter or margarine
¼ cup minced onion
1 pound hamburg
6 cups eggplant, cut into 2″ cubes
1 teaspoon salt (optional)
¼ teaspoon pepper
½ teaspoon Shaker Thyme
1 can tomato soup, undiluted
1 cup evaporated milk
2 teaspoons butter
½ cup bread crumbs

Melt the butter and brown onions and hamburg. Add eggplant, salt, pepper and thyme to taste. Cook over a low heat for 10 minutes. Stir in soup and milk. Pour into 2 quart casserole and top with buttered crumbs. Bake at 375° for 25-30 minutes.

This recipe is quite versatile. If you have fresh tomatoes, substitute them for the soup and milk. Or if you wish a meatless dish, just omit the hamburg. Then again you might add cheese as a topping instead of the bread crumbs. It is all up to your imagination or personal taste.

ONION AND CHEESE CASSEROLE

2 tablespoons butter or margarine
2 large Bermuda onions, sliced and separated
½ pound Swiss cheese, grated
Dash of pepper
1 can cream of chicken soup
¼ cup milk
Sliced French bread, as many slices as needed
   to cover top of casserole

Cook the onions in butter until soft, do not overcook. Pour onions into shallow casserole and cover evenly with cheese. Sprinkle with pepper. Heat soup and milk together until smooth. Pour over onion mixture. Cut through mixture with knife so that the sauce will go all through. Place buttered bread over the top and cover with foil. Bake covered for 1 hour at 350°.

SUMMER SQUASH CASSEROLE

2 pounds summer squash,* sliced
1 cup water
1 teaspoon salt
½ teaspoon sugar
4 tablespoons butter
1 cup grated cheddar cheese
2 eggs, slightly beaten
1 cup sour cream
1 medium onion, finely chopped
1/3 cup grated Parmesan cheese
Salt and pepper to taste
1 cup bread crumbs
3 tablespoons melted butter

Bring water to a boil; add salt, sugar and squash. Cook for 15 minutes. Drain and return to pan. Add the butter and mash. Stir in the cheese, eggs, cream and Parmesan cheese. Pour into buttered baking dish and top with crumbs and butter. Bake at 350° for 25 minutes.

*You may substitute zucchini for the summer squash if desired.

CHEESE AND SPINACH CASSEROLE

1 pound cottage cheese
3 eggs, unbeaten
¼ pound American cheese, cut in pieces
¼ cup butter or margarine
1 package frozen chopped spinach, partially thawed
3 tablespoons flour
Salt to taste

To the cottage cheese add eggs, American cheese and butter. Blend with as little mixing as possible until the mixture resembles a coarse batter. Add spinach and flour and stir until thoroughly blended. Pour into buttered 1½ quart casserole. Bake at 350° for 1 hour or until the top is golden. The top will resemble the crust.

MACARONI DELIGHT

1 cup elbow macaroni (before cooking)
1½ cups hot milk
1 cup soft bread crumbs
1½ cups grated cheese (use *your* favorite - we use
   sharp cheddar)
2 tablespoons chopped pimento
1 tablespoon minced onion
Salt and pepper to taste
3 eggs, separated

Cook the macaroni as directed on package. Pour the hot milk over the crumbs and mix in the cheese, pimento, onion, seasonings and egg yolks. Beat the egg whites until stiff and fold into the mixture. Add the macaroni. Bake at 350° for approximately 50 minutes.

MACARONI & CHEESE

1 8-ounce package elbow macaroni
¼ cup butter or margarine
¼ cup all-purpose flour
1 teaspoon salt (*optional*)
Dash of pepper
2 cups milk
2 cups cheddar cheese, grated

Preheat oven to 375°. Cook the macaroni according to directions on package, drain. Melt the butter in a saucepan. Remove from heat. Stir in flour and seasonings and stir until smooth. Return to heat and gradually add the milk, stirring as you add. Bring to boil, stirring constantly to keep from sticking. Reduce the heat and simmer for about another minute. Remove from heat and stir in the cheese and macaroni. Pour into a 1½ quart casserole. Sprinkle some cheese on top. Bake for approximately 20 minutes or until the cheese is golden brown.

For a quick and cheesy adaption of this dish, use a can of cheddar cheese soup and 1 cup of milk instead of 2 cups. This is good and cheesy.

VEGETABLES
AND
VEGETARIAN DISHES

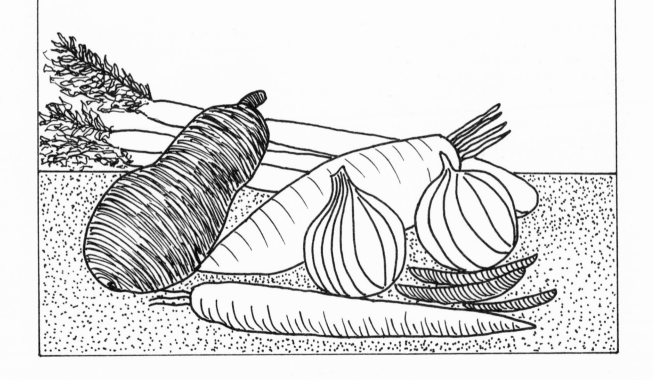

BAKED BEANS

7 cups beans
1 onion, chopped
½ cup brown sugar
½ cup white sugar
2 tablespoons molasses
2 level tablespoons salt
1 tablespoon dry mustard
1 good sized chunk salt pork, cut into big pieces

Two nights before you want to serve the beans, soak them in hot water overnight. In the morning parboil them. Drain well. Place the beans in a crock pot. Add the remaining ingredients and stir well. Set it on low overnight and most of the next day.

For smaller recipe cut this in half, although beans freeze well and are handy to have on hand in the freezer for unexpected company. Less beans, less than 7 cups, may be used with no trouble.

When we had the old wood stove we always had baked beans for Saturday dinner, but when the wood stove gave way to gas, it was deemed too expensive to bake beans. So for a short time our beans were baked by Carol Stinchfield of New Gloucester. A few years ago we received a "crock pot" for a Christmas present and have found that it makes delicious beans, almost as good as our old wood stove did!

SISTER MILDRED'S CREAMED POTATOES

Occasionally when we have boiled potatoes left over, we persuade Sister Mildred to make creamed potatoes for dinner. This dish was a common one for years when the community still had dairy cows and milk and cream as well as butter were always at hand. Somehow the butter and cream from the stores doesn't make the recipe taste the way it used to. It lacks the rich goodness of our own dairy products. However, this is still a delicious way to use potatoes.

1 heaping quart cold potatoes, diced
¼ pound butter or margarine
½ pint light cream

Melt the butter and add cream. Heat cream and butter until simmering. Add the potato and cook over low heat, stirring the cream into the potato as it cooks. When all the cream has been absorbed by the potato, turn into serving dish. Add dots of butter over the top and sprinkle with Shaker Fines Herbes. Serve as soon as it is ready.

Sister Mildred uses one of the cast iron frying pans, although a double boiler may also be used to cook the potatoes.

ZUCCHINI QUICHE

3 cups chopped zucchini (I use fresh, but frozen
   may be used)
1 cup chopped onion
1½ cloves garlic, minced
1½ tablespoons butter or margarine
1 tablespoon lemon juice
¼ teaspoon ginger
¼ teaspoon Shaker Basil
¼ teaspoon Shaker Oregano
¼ teaspoon Shaker Thyme
Salt & pepper to taste
3 eggs
2½ cups grated Swiss cheese

Melt the butter and saute the onions, garlic and
zucchini until tender. Beat the eggs and add
seasonings. Combine with the zucchini mixture. Add
the cheese. Pour into a buttered glass pie plate which
has been coated with very fine bread crumbs. Crumbs
may also be sprinkled on top. Bake at 350° for 40-45
minutes, or until a knife inserted into the center comes
out clean.

EGGPLANT PARMESAN

2/3 cup bread crumbs
1 tablespoon Parmesan cheese
½ garlic clove. minced
½ teaspoon Shaker Thyme
½ teaspoon Shaker Oregano

1 medium eggplant (about 1½ pounds)
2½ cups tomato sauce, your own or canned
¼ cup Parmesan cheese
½ teaspoon Shaker Basil
4 ounces grated Mozzarella cheese

Combine the bread crumbs with 1 tablespoon
Parmesan cheese, garlic, thyme and oregano. Set
aside. Peel and cut eggplant into slices approximately
½″ thick (usually this will make 8 slices). Place
eggplant in a buttered baking dish, 9″ x 13″, and
sprinkle with the seasoned bread crumbs. Bake in a
400° oven for 20-25 minutes or until tender. Remove
from the oven. Combine the tomato sauce with the ¼
cup Parmesan cheese and basil. Pour the sauce over the
eggplant covering all the edges. Sprinkle the
Mozzarell over top. Return to oven and bake for 15
minutes or until the cheese is melted and browned.
Sprinkle with Shaker Parsley and serve.

SAVORY CHEESE
AND ONION PIE

Pastry recipe for one 10″ pie.

10 ounces sharp cheddar cheese
2 tablespoons flour
2 large onions
4 tablespoons butter
1 teaspoons basil
2 large eggs
¾ cup light cream

Prepare the pastry as directed, line a 10″ pie dish and chill it. Grate the cheese and toss it with the flour. Melt the butter in a large skillet, slice the onions and saute them very gently in the butter until they begin to turn golden, about ½ hour. Spread about 1/3 of the cheese over the bottom of the pie dish, then spread the onions over it. In the butter that is left in the pan, heat the basil for a minute or two. Spread over the onions, then cover with the remaining cheese. Beat the eggs with the cream and pour it over the cheese. If you like nutmeg, sprinkle a little on top. Bake in a pre-heated oven for about 35-40 minutes, or until the top browns nicely.

Serves 6.

CORN SOUFFLE

This makes a very large casserole-type souffle, so if you have a small family cut the recipe in half.

3 cups milk
2 tablespoons butter
5 eggs
2½ teaspoons salt
2 teaspoons sugar
1 17-ounce can whole corn, drained

Heat the milk and butter together until the butter melts. In a two-quart casserole dish beat the eggs, salt and sugar together until well mixed. Stir in the corn.

Slowly add the milk to egg mixture and continue to beat constantly. Set the casserole in a pan of hot water. Make sure that the water comes halfway up the side of the casserole. Bake at 350° for 1 hour or until a knife inserted into the middle comes out clean. Serve immediately.

This makes a very good dish for company.

STUFFED BAKED ONIONS

3 pounds ground meat*
2 eggs
½ cup breadcrumbs
2 garlic cloves, crushed
1 teaspoon salt
1 teaspoon Shaker Marjoram
1 teaspoon Shaker Oregano
1 teaspoons Shaker Thyme
½ teaspoon pepper
10 large onions

Peel the onions and boil them for 10 minutes or until they are soft but not fully cooked. Cool them and begin to push the sections through the tops until you have many hollowed sections. Take the smaller sections, chop them into fine pieces and add to the remaining ingredients. Next stuff the onions. Place close together in a baking pan. Cover halfway up with chicken broth. Bake in a 350° oven for 1 hour. Drain and serve while very hot.

*Any type of ground meat will do. Hamburg, lamb, pork, chicken or turkey used alone or in combination, depending on your taste. All work well in this recipe.

STUFFED CABBAGES

1 pound ground meat (preferably lamb)
2 onions, chopped fine
¼ cup rice
¼ cup celery
¼ cup fresh parsley
2 teaspoons mint leaves, chopped
1 tablespoon olive oil
¼ cup beef stock
Salt & pepper to taste
1 cabbage
1 cup beef stock
1 egg
Juice of ½ lemon

Combine the meat, rice, onions, celery, parsley, mint leaves, olive oil, ¼ cup beef stock, salt and pepper. Place the cabbage in boiling water and cook just until softened. Roll some of the mixture on each of the cabbage leaves. Place each rolled leaf in a baking pan and dot each one with butter. Add 1 cup beef stock to whole rolls. Beat the egg with lemon juice and add it to the pan juices, beating constantly. Simmer for 40-45 minutes until rice is done.

HERBED CREAMED CABBAGE

1 medium-sized young cabbage with outer leaves removed
2 tablespoons butter or margarine
2 tablespoons flour
1 cup milk

Core and shred the cabbage. Drop into salted, rapidly boiling water. Boil for 5 minutes keeping it at a rapid boil. Melt the butter and add the flour, stirring to make a smooth mixture. Slowly add milk to flour mixture and stir constantly to make it smooth. Cover over low heat until thick enough for a sauce. Continue to cook for about 2 minutes. Add 1 tablespoon Shaker Caraway Seeds. Combine the cabbage and sauce. Heat and serve.

SCALLOPED TOMATOES

2½ cups canned tomatoes
2 tablespoons chopped onion
1 teaspoon salt (optional)
1 teaspoon sugar
1 cup soft bread crumbs, finely crumbled
3 tablespoons butter or margarine

Combine the tomatoes, onions and seasonings together. Pour into a buttered 1-quart casserole. Top with crumbs and dot with butter. Bake at 400° for 25 minutes or until browned.

SHAKER
STEWED TOMATO

1 quart tomatoes
½ cup light cream or rich milk
1 tablespoon sugar
¼ teaspoon baking soda
¼ teaspoon Shaker Bouquet Garni
¼ cup cracker crumbs*
1 tablespoon butter or margarine

Heat tomatoes. Add the cream and baking soda. Allow to simmer several minutes. Add the cracker crumbs. Simmer until cracker crumbs have swelled. Add the sugar, salt and Bouquet Garni. Just before serving add the butter; allow to melt. If you wish you may add a dollop of ketchup.

This is a very old Shaker recipe and has been used by all the Communities where it has always been a great favorite.

*Use saltines rolled fine. If using saltless crackers, increase salt a little more than stated.

BASIL TOMATOES

4 or 5 well-developed tomatoes, cut in half, unpeeled
¾ cup sharp cheese, grated (we prefer sharp cheddar)
½ cup fine bread crumbs
Dash of salt
Dash of pepper (freshly ground is superior)
½ teaspoon Shaker Basil

Arrange the tomato halves in a shallow baking dish. A glass casserole dish that is not too deep is fine. Place the tomatoes closely together. Sprinkle a little sugar lightly over the tomatoes. Mix together cheese, bread crumbs, salt, pepper and basil. Blend thoroughly and spoon over the tomatoes. Bake uncovered for 30 minutes at 375°.

ZUCCHINI FINGERS WITH
HERBS & CAPERS

8 small zucchini, unpeeled and left whole
   (about ¼ pound each)
6 tablespoons oil
2 tablespoons wine vinegar
1 clove garlic, minced
1 small onion, grated
Lettuce leaves
4 small tomatoes, peeled and cubed

½ small green pepper, cut into ¼" strips
1 tablespoon capers, rinsed and drained
1 green onion, minced
1 teaspoon Shaker Parsley
1 teaspoon Shaker Basil
 Salt and pepper to taste

Steam the whole zucchinis for 5-8 minutes or until tender-crisp. Cut in half lengthwise and then into quarters, making finger-shaped sticks. Mix oil, vinegar, garlic and onion together. Pour half of mixture over zucchini fingers. Cover and marinate for 4 hours in the refrigerator. When ready to serve lift zucchini out of marinade with slotted spoon and arrange on lettuce leaves. To the other half of the vinaigrette sauce and chopped tomatoes, green peppers, green onion, capers, parsley, basil, salt and pepper. Pour over the zucchini and lettuce and serve.

Dorothy Brown of California brought this recipe to us several years ago when she first began her volunteer work here at the Village.

BROCCOLI IN
ROSEMARY BUTTER

1 head broccoli
4 ounces butter
¼ teaspoon Shaker Rosemary, crumbled

Cook broccoli until just tender in boiling salted water. Drain and separate into flowerets. Melt the butter in skillet and allow to begin to brown. Add rosemary and pour herbed butter over broccoli.

Serves 4.

OMELET SOUFFLE

3 tablespoons butter or margarine
3 tablespoons flour
¾ teaspoon salt
⅛ teaspoon pepper
½ teaspoon Shaker Fines Herbes
1 cup milk
6 eggs, separated

In a heavy saucepan melt the butter. Blend in the flour, salt, pepper and Fines Herbes. Add the milk and cook slowly, stirring until thickened. Beat the egg whites until stiff. Then beat yolks until they are thick and lemon colored. Stir the first mixture into the yolks and blend thoroughly. Fold into egg whites. Pour into a 3-quart casserole and set in a pan of hot water. Allow the water to come halfway up the casserole dish. Bake at 350° for 35-40 minutes, or until a knife inserted in the center comes out clean. Serve at once.

A nice variation is:

CHEESE SOUFFLE

Prepare omelet as above but add ¼ teaspoon dry mustard and 1 cup of sharp cheddar cheese to the hot sauce. Stir until the cheese is melted. Proceed as directed with the above omelet souffle.

CABBAGE SLAW

Cabbage grows well in our gardens and we always have a good supply for the winter. Our favorite variety is the regular winter white cabbage, although we have been successful in raising the purple as well. Boiled cabbage is a favorite and it is one vegetable that we use very often. The cole slaw used here is a good way to use the young cabbage during the late summer and early fall, as cabbage stored in the cellar tends to yellow a bit.

4 cups cabbage, chopped (use only the firm part
  of the cabbage, discard outer leaves)
½ cup mayonnaise
3 tablespoons sour cream
2 teaspoons Shaker Tarragon Vinegar
1 teaspoon prepared mustard
1 teaspoon sugar
Dash of salt
¼ teaspoon Shaker Celery Seed
¼ teaspoon pepper
½ teaspoon Shaker Dill

Cover the cabbage and refrigerate. Blend together mayonnaise, sour cream, tarragon vinegar and mustard. Chill in refrigerator. Mix together the sugar, salt, celery seed, pepper and dill. Combine the 2 mixtures and pour over the cabbage. Mix well but lightly until the cabbage is well coated.

SABBATHDAY LAKE STUFFED EGGS

4 hard-cooked eggs, halved lengthwise
3 tablespoons butter or margarine
Salt & pepper to taste
½ teaspoon Shaker Chervil

Remove yolks from eggs and sieve. Blend butter, salt and pepper with the sieved egg yolk. Add chervil. Pipe egg yolk mixture into egg white halves and serve on a bed of watercress mayonnaise. Garnish with a few springs of fresh parsley. Serves 4.

MINTED SHAKER FRUIT CUP

Marinate a melange of seasonal fruits with a quantity of Shaker Spearmint in a cheese cloth bag. Serve well chilled with a garnish of fresh mint leaves.

ZESTY CARROTS

4 carrots
¼ cup butter or margarine
1 tablespoon Shaker Sweet Cicely Vinegar
Salt & pepper

Peel and cut the carrots into slices approximately ¼"
thick. Cook for 15 minutes, drain and then put the
carrots into the mixture of butter and Sweet Cicely
Vinegar. Cook gently until the carrots are soft. Add
salt and pepper to taste. Serve very hot.

SUMMER SQUASH

3 pounds small summer squash
Salt
¾ cup butter
2/3 cup finely chopped onion
1½ teaspoons paprika
½ teaspoon salt
¼ teaspoon pepper
1 tablespoon Shaker Dill
2 teaspoons Shaker Basil Vinegar
1 cup sour cream

Wash squash. Cut into quarters lengthwise and scoop
out all seeds. Cut squash into long, thin strips.

Sprinkle with salt and allow to stand for 1 hour.
Drain squash, squeezing gently to remove excess
moisture. In ½ cup of melted hot butter in a large
skillet saute onion until golden brown. Remove from
heat. Stir in squash, remaining butter, paprika, salt,
pepper, dill and Basil Vinegar. Cook uncovered over
medium heat, stirring occasionally, until the squash is
tender - approximately 15 minutes. Stir in the sour
cream and reheat gently. Serve at once.

SAVORY GREEN BEANS

1 package frozen green beans
2 tablespoons butter or margarine, melted and
   slightly browned
½ teaspoon Shaker Savory
Pinch of salt
Pinch of pepper
1 teaspoon lemon juice

Cook the beans as directed on the package. Add the
remaining ingredients together. Pour over the hot
beans and toss lightly. Serve at once.

Serves 3 to 4.

ASPARAGUS WITH
SWEET CICELY DRESSING

1½ pounds fresh asparagus
3 tablespoons olive oil
2 tablespoons Shaker Sweet Cicely Vinegar
Salt & pepper

Trim asparagus and wash under cold water. Cook in
boiling salted water for 2 minutes. Drain and refresh
under cold water. Set aside at room temperature. In a
bowl mix olive oil with Sweet Cicely Vinegar. Add
salt and pepper to taste. Mix well. Place the
asparagus on a platter large enough to accomodate all
and pour the dressing over them ½ hour before
serving.

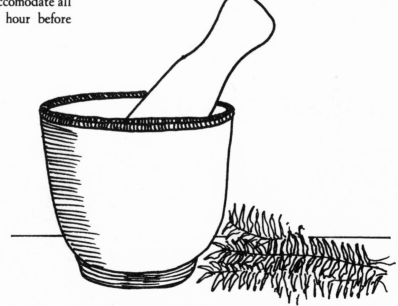

HERB COOKERY

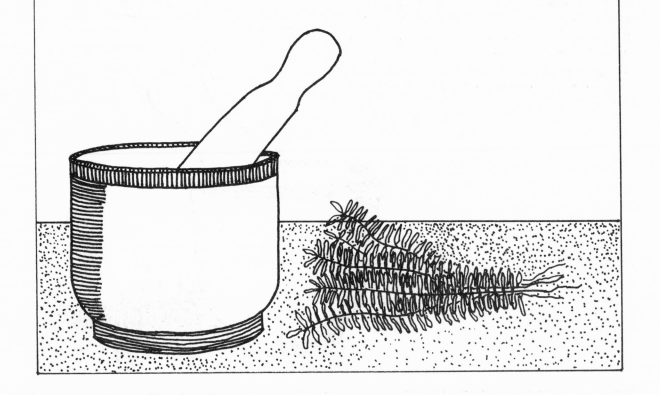

MINT BASTE

2 tablespoons chopped fresh mint leaves,
   or 1 tablespoon Shaker Mint Leaves
1 tablespoon Shaker Mint Vinegar
1 tablespoon honey

Mix ingredients together. Use this as a baste for lamb, pork or chicken.

MINT SAUCE

½ cup sugar
¼ teaspoon salt
½ cup water
1 cup Shaker Mint Vinegar
½ cup fresh chopped mint leaves,
   or ¼ cup Shaker Mint Leaves

Combine the sugar, salt and water. Add vinegar and bring to a boil. Simmer for 10 minutes. Pour over mint leaves and allow to set for 30 minutes. Serve this either hot or cold.

DILL SAUCE

¼ cup butter or margarine
4 tablespoons flour
Dash of salt (optional)
2 teaspoons Shaker Dill
2 cups milk

Melt butter over low heat and slowly stir in the flour. Stir until the mixture is a smooth paste. Add the salt and dill. Slowly add milk, stirring constantly, and cook approximately eight minutes, or until thickened. Stir to prevent sticking. Serve over boiled potatoes, scrambled eggs or fish.

HERB BUTTER FOR VEGETABLES

4 tablespoons butter or margarine
1 teaspoon of either Shaker Basil, Shaker Dill,
   Shaker Parsley or Shaker Thyme

Melt the butter and add the herb. Simmer for a minute or two. Pour over your favorite vegetable just before serving.

My favorite is dill poured over diced carrots. The parsley butter adds a lot to a plain boiled potato.

MINT CHUTNEY

1 cup mint leaves
2 cups raisins
1 teaspoon salt
¼ cup Shaker Mint Vinegar
Pinch of Cayenne

Put the mint leaves and the raisins twice through the mincer. Add the salt, mint vinegar and cayenne. Mix all the ingredients thoroughly. Fill small jars with the mixture. Press down well so that no air spaces are left.

This chutney requires no cooking, but it will not keep longer than a week or two. It is best to keep it in the refrigerator.

DILL DIP

2/3 cup salad dressing
2/3 cup sour cream
1 tablespoon minced onion
1 tablespoon Shaker Parsley
1 tablespoon Shaker Dill Seed
1 teaspoon salt

Mix in order given and serve with assorted vegetable sticks. Allow dill dip to season in refrigerator. The dill taste strengthens with time.

CARAWAY SPREAD

1 pound cheddar cheese, grated or cut into
   small pieces
½ cup beer
2 tablespoons butter or margarine
½ teaspoon garlic salt
1 tablespoon Shaker Caraway Seeds

Heat the cheese, beer and butter in a saucepan just until cheese melts, no more. Remove from heat. Add salt and caraway seeds. Beat mixture with egg beater until thoroughly blended. Pour into small dishes and refrigerate until ready to use. Serve with rye bread or wheat thins for delicious snacks.

WATERCRESS MAYONNAISE

12 ounces mayonnaise
3 ounces heavy cream
Juice of 1 whole lemon
1 bunch watercress
Salt
White pepper

In a blender or food processor, blend all ingredients together until smooth.

MUSTARD HERB BUTTER

½ cup butter or margarine
2 tablespoons prepared mustard
1 tablespoon chopped onion
1 tablespoon Shaker Parsley

Cream butter; beat in mustard and stir in onion and

parsley. This is good when served on crackers as a canape or small toasted rounds of bread. This may be topped with half an olive.

SESAME HERB TOAST

1 egg, well beaten
½ cup soft butter or margarine
1 tablespoon flour
2 tablespoons sesame seeds
¼ teaspoon Shaker Marjoram
¼ teaspoon Shaker Basil
¼ teaspoon Shaker Rosemary
1 tablespoon dried chives

Mix all the above ingredients together in a bowl. Use rounds of bread or thin slices of unbaked bread, sliced thin. When mixture is thoroughly mixed, spread on rounds; place on cookie sheets and bake at 350° until slightly browned. Good served with soup course.

MINTED
CUCUMBER SALAD

5-7 cucumbers
½ cup olive oil
¼ cup Shaker Mint Vinegar
1 tablespoon sugar
Salt & pepper
Mint leaves, fresh or dried Shaker Mint Leaves

Slice the cucumbers as thin as possible. Cover with a dressing consisting of the olive oil and Mint Vinegar. Add sugar, salt and pepper. Set aside, in the refrigerator, for at least 3 hours before serving. Just before serving, add a few uncut fresh mint leaves.

HERBED
POTATO SALAD

4 potatoes
2 teaspoons Shaker Caraway Seed
3 teaspoons oil
1 small onion, chopped
Salt & pepper
2 teaspoons Shaker Chervil
2 teaspoons Shaker Parsley
3 tablespoons Shaker Sweet Cicely Vinegar
¼ cup salad dressing

Peel potatoes and boil them. Drain and cool. Cut into cubes and marinate them in oil, onion, salt and pepper. Add the chervil and parsley to the potatoes and toss them gently. Mix in the Sweet Cicely Vinegar and salad dressing. Serve either warm or chilled.

PIES

SISTER MARIE'S PIE CRUST

1 cup vegetable shortening or lard
2½ cups flour
1 teaspoon salt
4-5 tablespoons cold water

Sift the flour and salt together. Mix in the shortening until the pieces are the size of peas. Gradually add the cold water, 1 tablespoon at a time. Do not mix too much. Roll out onto a lightly floured board. Makes enough for two 9″ crusts.

SISTER MARIE'S APPLE PIE

6 large apples (We use whatever is in season. In the early part of the fall we use MacIntosh, and then as winter comes on, we like Cortlands.)
1¼ cups sugar
¼ teaspoon nutmeg
½ teaspoon cinnamon
Pastry for two 9″ crusts

Peel and cut apples into thin slices. Layer the apples in a pastry lined 9″ pie plate. After using approximately half the apples, use half of the sugar and spices, sprinkling them over the apples. Fill with remaining apples and top with remaining sugar and spices. Top with small dots of butter. Add top crust and seal well. Make vents in top of pie for steam to escape. Bake for 15 minutes at 425°. Reduce heat to 350°. Continue baking for 40-45 minutes. Test apples for doneness.

Apple pie is a pretty basic recipe for all of New England, so this is not very different from what the average person would make. This, however, is the one that is made here at Sabbathday Lake. Because we have a large orchard of approximately 2,500 trees, we use a lot of apples. Since Brother Delmer started the commercial side of the orchard in 1912, it has been added to over the years. The main crop consists of the MacIntosh, Cortland, and Red and Yellow Delicious varieties, but we also have many 19th century varieties, including the Yellow Transparencies, Ben Davis, Winter Banana, Strawberry, Northern Spy, and Baldwin.

Just below the apple orchard, behind the old Meeting House, we have a small pear orchard and several cherry trees. Brother Delmer left the community well provided for as far as fruit goes.

SHAKER APPLE PIE

3 cups apples, peeled and sliced
2/3 cup sugar
1 tablespoon cream
1 tablespoon Shaker Rose Water
Pastry for two 9″ crusts

Slice apples into mixing bowl and add the sugar, cream and rose water. Mix thoroughly so that the rose water will be distributed evenly. Line a pie dish with pastry. Fill with the apple mixture and cover with top crust in which a few small vents have been slashed for steam to escape. Brush with a very little rose water mixed with milk. Bake in a moderate oven, 350°, for 50 minutes.

BLUEBERRY PIE

1 quart blueberries
1½ cups sugar
2 tablespoons flour
Cinnamon
Pastry for two 9″ crusts

Mix flour and sugar together. Combine with blueberries thoroughly. Turn into pastry lined pie plate. Top with dots of butter and lightly sprinkle cinnamon over the filling. Cover with top crust. Bake at 450° for 10 minutes. Reduce heat to 350° and continue to bake for 50 minutes.

CHERRY PIE

2 cups canned unsweetened cherries
2 scant tablespoons corn starch
3 heaping tablespoons sugar
Dash of salt *(optional)*

1 full, running over, cup cherry juice
1 tablespoon butter

Drain the cherries, but save the juice. Combine cornstarch, sugar and salt. Gradually add cherry juice and stir constantly. Cook slowly over low heat until mixture is smooth and thickened. Add butter and cherries. Let cool. Pour into pastry lined 9″ pie plate. Cover with top crust and bake at 450° for 15 minutes. Reduce heat to 350° and bake for 25 minutes longer.

Since we have several cherry trees set out by Elder William, we usually have an abundance of cherries in the freezer for pies and puddings.

SQUASH PIE

2 cups strained squash
½ cup brown sugar
½ teaspoon salt
1 teaspoon ginger
½ teaspoon allspice
½ teaspoon nutmeg
½ teaspoon cinnamon
2 eggs, beaten
1½ cups milk
Pastry for one 9″ pie shell

Mix sugar, salt and spices together. Blend well. Combine with squash. To the beaten eggs add milk and stir well. Blend into squash mixture. Pour into pastry lined pie plate. Preheat oven and bake at 425° for 20 minutes. Reduce heat to 375° and continue to bake pie for 40 minutes longer, or until the tip of a knife inserted into the center comes out clean.

PINEAPPLE PIE FILLING

2 cups crushed pineapple
2 eggs, well beaten
1 cup sugar
1 tablespoon corn starch
Pastry for 2 crusts

Beat the sugar into the eggs. Add in the pineapple and corn starch. Mix thoroughly. Pour into pastry lined pie plate. Dot with small dots of butter. Top with pastry and bake at 450° for 15 minutes. Reduce heat to 350° and bake for 20 minutes longer.

PUMPKIN PIE

2 eggs, slightly beaten
¾ cup sugar
1½ teaspoons cinnamon
½ teaspoon nutmeg
½ teaspoon ginger
¼ teaspoon cloves
½ teaspoon salt
2 cups pumpkin, cooked and sieved
3 tablespoons molasses
2 6-ounce cans evaporated milk
Pastry for one 9" pie shell

In a large bowl combine eggs, sugar, spices, salt, pumpkin, molasses and evaporated milk. Stir with a wooden spoon until mixture is smooth. Line pie dish with pastry and fill with pumpkin mixture. Bake in a preheated 400° oven for 55-60 minutes or until the tip of a sharp knife inserted in the center comes out clean.

RHUBARB PIE

2 tablespoons flour
1 very full cup sugar
1 egg, well beaten
2 cups diced rhubarb
Pastry for 1 pie

Combine flour, sugar and egg. Add rhubarb. Mix well. Pour into pastry lined pie plate. Dot with butter and cover with pastry. Bake at 450° for 15 minutes, then lower oven to 350° for 25 minutes, or until the pie is well browned.

This is delicious.

CUSTARD PIE

1 egg, separated
½ cup sugar
¼ teaspoon salt
¼ teaspoon nutmeg
1 teaspoon vanilla
2 large eggs
2½ cups milk
Pastry for one 9″ pie

Beat the egg white until stiff. Add the sugar, salt, nutmeg and vanilla. Blend well. Then add the eggs and egg yolk. Beat together. Warm the milk and add to the egg mixture. Combine well. Pour into unbaked pastry shell and place in a preheated 450° oven. After placing pie in oven, reset to 425° and bake for 30-35 minutes. If you feel uncertain about time, the pie is done when the center is set and does not shake.

This recipe came to Sister Mildred with the electric light bill. Recipes like this tend to soften the blow of the bill.

KEY LIME PIE

4 eggs, separated
1 can condensed milk
½ cup lime juice
6 tablespoons sugar
½ teaspoon cream of tartar
Pastry for one 9″ pie

Preheat oven to 350°. Beat egg yolks. Add condensed milk and lime juice. Beat until thick. Beat 1 egg white until stiff and fold into mixture. Pour into baked pie shell.

For the topping, beat the remaining 3 egg whites. Blend in sugar and cream of tartar. Beat until stiff and peaks form. Bake until the egg whites are golden brown.

BLENDER
KEY LIME PIE

1 3-ounce package lime gelatin
½ cup boiling water
1 lime peel, grated
½ cup fresh lime juice
2 eggs, separated
1 can condensed milk
1 9″ pastry shell, pre-baked

Into blender put the lime gelatin, boiling water and grated rind. Blend for 20 seconds on high. Add the lime juice and egg yolks. Cover and blend. Uncover and add the condensed milk. Cover and blend together. Beat the egg whites and fold them into the lime mixture. Refrigerate until the mixture thickens slightly, but not too much. Turn into baked pie shell and refrigerate until set.

SISTER ELIZABETH'S LEMON PIE

3 tablespoons corn starch
1½ cups sugar
½ cup lemon juice
1 teaspoon salt
3 eggs, separated
1½ cups boiling water

Combine corn starch, sugar, lemon juice and salt. Beat egg yolks until light and frothy. Add egg yolks to corn starch mixture. Gradually add the boiling water to the above mixture. Heat to the boiling point in double boiler. Boil gently for 4 minutes stirring constantly. Pour into baked shell.

MERINGUE

Beat the egg whites until stiff, but not dry. Gradually beat in 6 tablespoons sugar. Spread meringue over pie, being careful to seal all edges. This is done by spreading the meringue to edges of crust. Bake at 400° for 7-9 minutes or until meringue is golden brown.

SHAKER LEMON PIE

2 lemons
2 cups sugar
4 eggs, beaten
Pastry for 2 crusts

Slice the lemons paper thin, rind and all. Place in a bowl and mix in the sugar. Let this stand for 2 hours or longer. Line a 9″ pie plate with pastry. Add the eggs to lemon mixture. Blend well. Pour into pie shell. Cover with top crust and cut air vents in top. Be sure to crimp the edges to prevent leaking. Bake at 450° for 15 minutes. Reduce the heat to 350° for 30 minutes or until a knife inserted in the center comes out clean.

SHAKER APPLE DUMPLINGS

4 large, crisp apples (we prefer Cortlands)
½ cup sugar
2 tablespoons cream
1 tablespoon Shaker Rose Water
Pastry for 2 crusts

Mix together the sugar, cream and rose water. Set aside. Peel and core the apples. Wrap the apples in pastry, leaving enough opening at the top to fill with mixture. Evenly distribute the mixture among the 4 apples. Bring the corners together and press so they stay together. Prick the pastry in several places. Place in a 9″ baking dish. Bake in a preheated 450° oven for 15 minutes or until well browned.

CAKES

ALMOND CREAM CAKE

1 cup butter or margarine
1½ cups sugar
2 cups flour
¼ cup milk
5 egg whites
1 teaspoon almond extract
½ teaspoon baking powder

Beat butter and sugar together. Beat in egg whites and almond extract. Sift dry ingredients together. Add the flour mixture, alternating with the milk to egg mixture. Bake in 2 greased 8″ tins at 350° for 30-35 minutes.

CREAM FILLING

½ cup soft butter or margarine
3½ cups sifted confectioner's sugar
3 tablespoons hot milk
1 teaspoon almond extract
1 cup crushed almonds

In a medium bowl combine the sugar, butter, milk and almond extract. Beat until fluffy. Gradually add in the almonds.

Fill between the layers and the top and sides of the cake with the cream filling.

This is a very old recipe that was a specialty of Eldress Prudence Stickney. This was made for very special occasions. Eldress Prudence had a great host of celebrated friends who were served this cake, including such notables as Governor & Mrs. Lewis O. Barrows of Maine, Governor Percival P. Baxter and his sister Madeleine Baxter Tomlinson, also of Maine, as well as President & Mrs. Herbert C. Hoover.

MOTHER ANN'S BIRTHDAY CAKE

1 cup butter or margarine
2 cups sugar
3 cups flour
½ cup cornstarch
3 teaspoons baking powder
1 cup milk
2 teaspoons Shaker Rose Water
12 egg whites, beaten
1 teaspoon salt

Beat butter and sugar into a smooth cream. Sift flour with cornstarch and baking powder. Add flour mixture in small amounts alternately with milk to butter mixture. Beat after each addition. Add Rose Water. Beat egg whites with the salt. Beat until stiff and lightly fold into the flour mixture. Bake in 3 8″ cake tins at 350° for 25 minutes.

When cool, fill between the layers with peach jelly and cover the cake with a white icing flavored with Rose Water.

CHOCOLATE CAKE

¼ cup butter
¼ cup shortening
2 cups sugar
1 teaspoon vanilla
2 eggs
¾ cup cocoa
1¾ cups unsifted flour
¾ teaspoon baking powder
⅛ teaspoon salt
1¾ cups milk

Grease and flour two 9″ round cake pans. Cream butter, shortening, sugar and vanilla until light and fluffy. Blend in eggs. Combine baking soda, cocoa, flour, baking powder and salt in bowl; add alternately with milk to batter. Blend well. Pour into prepared pans. Bake at 350° for 30-35 minutes or until cake tester inserted comes out clean. Cool in pans 5 minutes before removing.

SISTER ETHEL'S CHOCOLATE CAKE

1¾ cups cake flour
½ teaspoon salt
1 teaspoon baking soda
½ cup cocoa

1½ cups sugar
2/3 cup milk
2 eggs
½ cup butter or margarine
1 teaspoon vanilla

Cream the sugar and eggs together. Add milk, butter and vanilla. Sift the dry ingredients together and gradually add into the first mixture. Mix thoroughly. Bake in a square pan, 9″ x 9″, for 25 minutes at 375°. Serve with vanilla sauce.

DUTCH APPLE CAKE

1 cup sugar
2 eggs, beaten
½ cup milk
2 cups flour
2 heaping teaspoons baking powder
6-8 apples
½ cup butter or margarine, melted
½-¾ cup sugar
1 teaspoon cinnamon

Mix the sugar, eggs, milk, flour and baking powder together. Pour mixture in a 12″ x 16″ pan. Pare and slice the apples. Lay them on the cake batter real closely together. Now pour the melted butter over all and sprinkle the sugar which has been combined with the cinnamon. Bake in a moderate oven, 350°, until apples are tender. This should take 30-35 minutes.

OUR FAVORITE SPICE CAKE

2½ cups sifted cake flour
1 teaspoon double acting baking powder
1 teaspoon baking soda
¾ teaspoon salt
¾ teaspoon cinnamon
¾ teaspoon cloves
1 cup granulated sugar
2/3 cup brown sugar
½ cup shortening (room temperature)
1 cup buttermilk
2 eggs

Sift together the flour, baking powder, soda, salt, spices and granulated sugar. In a mixing bowl beat shortening enough to soften. Add the dry ingredients and mix well. The batter will be stiff. Then add brown sugar and 2/3 cup of buttermilk. Mix until flour mixture is dampened. Add eggs and remaining milk. Beat for approximately 2 minutes. Pour batter into two 9" layer cake pans. Bake in a moderate oven, 375°, for 25-30 minutes or until a tester inserted into the center of the cake comes out clean.

This cake is especially good with your favorite white icing or frosting. This recipe is very old and always a favorite here at Sabbathday Lake.

ELDRESS PRUDENCE'S AMBROSIA CAKE

2/3 cup butter or margarine
2 cups sugar
½ cup milk
3 cups flour
4 eggs
1 teaspoon baking soda
2 teaspoons cream of tartar

Cream butter and sugar together. Add the eggs one at a time, beating thoroughly after each egg is added. Sift all dry ingredients together and add them alternately with the milk to the sugar-egg mixture. Bake in 2 greased 8" tins for 30-35 minutes. When cool, fill with the following.

FILLING

1 egg, well beaten
½ pint heavy cream, whipped
1 cup grated coconut
½ cup sugar
Juice and rind (grated) of one orange

Add together the above ingredients and spread between the layers and on the top of the cake.

BROTHER WAYNE'S APPLESAUCE CAKE

2½ cups flour
1¾ cups brown sugar
½ teaspoon baking powder
1½ teaspoon baking soda
1 teaspoon salt
1 teaspoon cinnamon
½ teaspoon cloves
½ teaspoon allspice
½ teaspoon nutmeg
½ teaspoon ginger
½ cup shortening
1¾ cups applesauce
3 eggs
1 cup raisins
1 cup nuts, chopped (*optional*)

Sift flour, sugar, baking powder, baking soda, salt and spices together. Add shortening and applesauce and beat just enough to combine. Add in eggs and heat until well combined. Fold in the raisins and nuts. Pour into a greased and floured 13" x 9" x 2" baking pan. Bake at 350° for 45 minutes or until a tester inserted in the center comes out clean. Serve as is or frost with Rose Water Frosting.

ROSEWATER FROSTING

4 cups confectioner's sugar, sifted
¼ cup light cream
1 tablespoon Shaker Rose Water

In a medium bowl combine all the ingredients. Stir until smooth. Spread over cake, cupcakes or cookies.

This is especially good with Mother Ann's Birthday Cake and Brother Wayne's Applesauce Cake.

SPONGE CAKE
(Hot Milk Cake)

1 cup sugar
2 eggs
½ cup hot milk
1 teaspoon butter or margarine
1 heaping cup flour
1 teaspoon baking powder
1 teaspoon vanilla

Melt the butter in hot milk. Sift flour and baking powder together. Add to hot milk. Stir well. Add the eggs, sugar and vanilla. Mix well. Bake in a greased tube pan at 350° for 25-30 minutes.

SISTER FRANCES' CHEESE CAKE

1¾ cups graham cracker crumbs
4 tablespoons butter or margarine
1 teaspoon cinnamon
2 tablespoons sugar
1 pound cream cheese
3 eggs
½ cup sugar
1 teaspoon vanilla
1 pint sour cream
½ cup sugar
1 teaspoon vanilla

Combine the graham cracker crumbs, butter, cinnamon and sugar. Press out into spring-form pan. Beat together the cream cheese, eggs, sugar and vanilla. Pour into crust and bake for 25 minutes at 350°. Remove from oven and allow cake to cool slightly, approximately 10 minutes. While the cake is cooling, mix the sour cream, sugar and vanilla. Pour over the cooled cake. Try to have it evenly spread over entire cake. Return to oven and bake at 450° for 10 minutes.

You may use your favorite topping. Canned pie filling, especially cherry, is very good. The cake is also good without topping.

I always make this for Sister Mildred's birthday. It really is her favorite cake.

SISTER DELLA'S PINEAPPLE UPSIDE DOWN CAKE

1/3 cup butter or margarine, melted
½ cup brown sugar, firmly packed
Pineapple slices
Maraschino cherries (*optional*)
2 eggs
6 tablespoons juice from pineapple
1 teaspoon vanilla
1 cup flour
1/3 teaspoon baking powder
¼ teaspoon salt

Preheat oven to 350°. In a 10" baking dish, evenly pour the melted butter and sprinkle the brown sugar evenly over the butter. Arrange the pineapple slices over this mixture. Garnish with cherries if desired. Beat eggs until thick and lemon colored. Gradually beat in the sugar. Add juice and vanilla and beat all together. Sift together flour, salt and baking powder. Add to the egg mixture and pour all over fruit. Bake for 45 minutes or until tester inserted in the center comes out clean. Immediately turn the cake upside down on a large plate. Leave pan over the cake for approximately 10 minutes so it easily removes from the cooking pan. Serve warm with whipped cream.

SISTER ELSIE'S FRUIT CAKE

1¼ cups shortening
1½ cups sugar
6 eggs
1 teaspoon baking powder
3 cups all-purpose flour
Raisins, nuts and citron (not to exceed 4 cups)
1 teaspoon cinnamon
½ cup cream, or evaporated milk

Cream shortening well. Slowly add sugar. Then add the eggs one at a time. Beat well. Sift baking powder, flour and cinnamon. Add flour mixture to sugar-egg mixture. Add fruits and nuts, and last of all the cream. Bake in a large greased tube pan at 350° for 1½ hours.

You may decorate the cake before baking with cherries and nuts. You may also bake this in 2 loaf pans. Makes a 5-pound cake.

Not a cake to be made often, but good for special occasions.

SPICE CUP CAKES

1 egg
1 cup sugar
2 cups flour
1 teaspoon baking soda
1 teaspoon cinnamon
1 teaspoon cloves
½ cup shortening, melted
1 cup sour milk
½ cup raisins, chopped
½ cup nuts, chopped (*optional*)

Mix egg with sugar. Sift together the flour, baking soda, cinnamon and cloves. Sift ingredients twice. Add the dry ingredients to the egg mixture. Beat together thoroughly. Add melted shortening which has been cooled. Beat well again. Add the milk and beat until the mixture is smooth. Add the raisins and nuts. Mix well. Bake in greased muffin tins in a moderate oven, 350°-375°, for 20-25 minutes.

JELLY ROLL

8 eggs, separated
1 1/3 cups confectioner's sugar
1 1/3 cups flour
½ teaspoon salt
1 teaspoon baking powder

Beat the egg yolks and sugar together until light. Add the dry ingredients. Beat the egg whites until very stiff. Gently fold into the first mixture. Bake in a greased 8" x 14" pan at 375° for 12-15 minutes. As soon as it comes out of the oven, turn it out on a wet towel. Spread with jelly and roll up. Dust the top with confectioner's sugar.

BOILED CAKE

1 cup raisins
1 cup water
½ cup shortening
1 cup sugar
1 teaspoon cinnamon
½ teaspoon cloves
½ teaspoon nutmeg
1 egg, beaten
1 teaspoon baking soda
½ teaspoon salt
2 scant cups flour
Fruit & nuts for topping

In a large saucepan combine the raisins, water, shortening, sugar and spices. Boil for 20 minutes and cool. Then add in the remaining ingredients. Pour into a greased tube pan and decorate with candied cherries and pecan halves. Bake at 350° or 375° for 45 minutes.

LEMON FILLING AND FROSTING

½ cup butter or margarine
1 cup sugar
1½ tablespoons flour
Grated rind and juice of 2 lemons
3 egg yolks, beaten
1 cup boiling water

Cream butter and sugar together. Blend in flour. Add rind, juice of lemons and egg yolks. Add boiling water and cook in the top of a double boiler until thick. Cool before spreading.

This recipe makes enough to fill and frost 1 layer cake, or to fill about 2 jelly rolls.

This recipe came to us from Regina Laudis, a Benedictine abbey of the Primitive Observance situated in Bethlehem, Connecticut. We have shared a long and loving relationship with the Sisters there over 20 years.

FUDGE FROSTING

4 squares unsweetened chocolate
½ cup soft butter or margarine
6½ cups sifted confectioner's sugar
⅛ teaspoon salt
½ cup hot cream
1 teaspoon very strong coffee

Melt the chocolate, being careful not to burn. Set aside and allow to cool. In a bowl combine the sugar, butter, salt and cream. Beat until mixture is smooth. If frosting is too thick, add more cream in very small amounts until desired consistency is reached.

Makes enough to fill and frost an 8" or 9" two-layer cake.

SEVEN MINUTE FROSTING

2 egg whites
1½ cups sugar
1/3 cup water
1 tablespoon light corn syrup
1 teaspoon vanilla extract

In top of double boiler, combine the egg whites, sugar, water and corn syrup. With mixer beat for approximately 1 minute just to combine the ingredients. Cook over rapidly boiling water beating constantly, for approximately 7 minutes, or until stiff peaks form when beater is raised. Remove from heat and add vanilla. Continue beating until frosting is thick enough to spread, about 2 minutes.

Makes enough to fill and frost an 8″ layer cake.

GINGERBREAD

2½ cups flour
1½ teaspoons baking soda
¼ teaspoon ground cloves
1 teaspoon cinnamon
1 teaspoon ginger
½ cup shortening
½ cup sugar
1 egg, unbeaten
1 cup molasses
1 cup hot water

Sift flour, salt and spices together. Cream shortening with sugar. Add the egg and beat until light and fluffy. Beat in molasses. Alternately and slowly beat in flour mixture and hot water. Bake at 350° for 35 minutes or until the middle is firm. Serve warm with whipped cream.

It is also good served plain.

COOKIES

JUMBLE COOKIES

1 cup shortening
2 teaspoons salt
1½ teaspoons cinnamon
¼ teaspoon nutmeg
2 cups sugar
3 eggs, beaten
1 teaspoon vanilla
2 cups raisins
1 cup warm water
1 teaspoon baking soda
3½ cups flour
1 teaspoon baking powder

Add water to raisins and simmer over very low heat for 4-5 minutes. Remove from heat and cool. Blend in the baking soda. Set aside. Blend shortening, salt and spices; gradually add in sugar. Add beaten eggs, vanilla and cooled raisins. Sift flour and baking powder together and add to mixture. Chill dough for approximately 10 minutes in refrigerator. Drop by half tablespoons on greased baking sheet. Bake at 375° for 12-15 minutes or until tester comes out clean.

CRUNCH JUMBLE COOKIES

1¼ cups flour
½ teaspoon baking soda
¼ teaspoon salt
½ cup butter or margarine, softened
1 cup sugar
1 egg
1 teaspoon vanilla
2 cups Rice Krispies
1 16-ounce bag chocolate morsels
1 cup raisins (optional)

Combine all ingredients together. Mix well. Drop by level tablespoon onto a greased cookie sheet. Bake approximately 12 minutes at 350°. Remove immediately from baking sheets. Yields approximately 40 cookies, 2½" size.

SOFT MOLASSES COOKIES

2¼ cups flour plus 1 tablespoon
2 teaspoons baking soda
¼ teaspoon salt
1 teaspoon ginger
1 teaspoon cinnamon
½ cup sugar

½ cup shortening
1 egg
½ cup molasses
½ cup warm water

Sift together the flour, baking soda, salt and spices. Set aside. Cream together the sugar and shortening. Then add the egg and molasses. Beat until mixture is smooth. Add flour mixture alternately with warm water, a little at a time, beginning and ending with flour mixture. Drop by teaspoons on ungreased cookie sheet. Bake at 375° for 12-15 minutes or until tester comes out clean.

ICE BOX COOKIES

1 cup butter or margarine, softened
2 cups brown sugar
2 eggs, slightly beaten
¼ teaspoon salt
¼ teaspoon nutmeg
1 teaspoon baking soda
3 cups flour
1 cup nuts, finely chopped
1 teaspoon vanilla

Cream softened butter with brown sugar. Add eggs and mix well. Then sift together the salt, nutmeg, baking soda and flour. Add to the first mixture. Then add nuts and vanilla. Knead well with hands and place in a loaf pan which has been lined with waxed paper and place in the refrigerator overnight. Slice thin and bake in hot oven, 400°, for 7-10 minutes. This mixture will keep in refrigerator for 3 weeks and can be cut and freshly baked when needed.

DROPPED COOKIES

2/3 cup cooking oil
1 cup sugar
¼ cup molasses
1 egg
2 cups flour
2 teaspoons baking soda
½ teaspoon cloves
½ teaspoon ginger
1 teaspoon cinnamon
¼ teaspoon salt

Beat together oil, sugar, molasses and egg. Mix thoroughly. Sift together the flour, baking soda, spices and salt. Add to the first mixture. Mix together well. The dough will be stiff, but it must be that way. If you find that you can't mix thoroughly with a spoon, do not hesitate to use your hands. Drop by spoonfuls, teaspoon if you like small cookies, tablespoon if you like large cookies. Bake at 375°, 10 minutes for small cookies and 12-13 for large ones. These will harden after they are taken out of oven, so if you think that they look underdone, do not hesitate to remove them just the same.

These cookies were a favorite at our bicentennial conference.

RUTH'S FRUIT COOKIES

2 cups sugar
¾ cup shortening
3 cups flour
3 eggs
1 teaspoon baking soda
½ cup rich milk
1 cup raisins
1 cup dried fruits
½ cup chopped nuts
½ teaspoon cinnamon
½ teaspoon nutmeg

Thoroughly combine sugar and eggs. Add shortening and mix until well blended. Add baking soda and spices to flour. Add flour mixture to the first mixture and mix thoroughly. Add milk and gradually add in the fruits and nuts. Spread mixture on greased cookie sheet, ½" thick. Sprinkle generously with sugar and bake approximately 20 minutes at 350°. Cut into squares. This keeps well and makes an excellent Christmas gift.

HALF-MOON COOKIES

1 teaspoon baking soda
3 cups flour
1 teaspoon baking powder
½ teaspoon salt

¾ cup shortening
2 eggs
1½ cups sugar
1 teaspoon vanilla
1 cup sour milk

Mix milk with dry ingredients. Beat until smooth. Drop by the teaspoonful onto a greased cookie sheet. Bake at 350° for 10-12 minutes. When cool, frost half chocolate and half vanilla.

FROSTING

¾ cup butter or margarine
1 16-ounce box confectioner's sugar
1 teaspoon vanilla
Milk enough for spreading consistency

Combine the above ingredients together. Beat until smooth. Frost half of each cookie with frosting. To the remaining frosting add 1 tablespoon cocoa and then frost the remaining sides of each cookie.

FILLED COOKIES

1 cup sugar
½ cup shortening
1 egg
½ cup milk

3½ cups flour
2 teaspoons baking powder
1 teaspoon vanilla

Cream sugar into shortening. Beat in egg. Add milk, flour, baking powder and vanilla. Mix together. Roll out thin and place a spoonful of dough on greased cookie sheet. Put a rounded teaspoon of filling on top of first cookie. Wet the edges of bottom cookie so the top will stick to the bottom. Place second cookie on top and seal together. Bake at 450° for 8 minutes.

FILLING

½ cup raisins
½ cup sugar
½ cup water
1 teaspoon flour

Combine the ingredients and cook until thick. Cool before filling cookies.

RUTH'S HERMITS

1 cup sugar
1 egg
½ cup molasses
½ cup shortening
½ cup cold water
2½ cups flour plus 2 tablespoons
1 teaspoon baking soda, level
¼ teaspoon salt
½ teaspoon cinnamon
½ teaspoon nutmeg
Nuts and raisins

Combine the sugar and egg together. Add the shortening and cream the mixture. Combine the molasses and cold water together. Gradually add to the sugar mixture. Then add the nuts and raisins. Bake on ungreased cookie sheet. You may either put the batter all on the cookie sheet and cut into squares or you may drop from a spoon and form round cookies. Sprinkle cookies with sugar and bake at 350°.

APPLE BROWNIES

¼ cup butter or margarine, melted
1 cup sugar
1 egg, beaten
2 medium-sized apples, chopped
1 cup flour
½ teaspoon baking powder
½ teaspoon baking soda
½ teaspoon cinnamon
Nuts (optional)

Sift the dry ingredients together. Cream sugar with beaten egg. Add butter and dry ingredients to sugar mixture. Add in the chopped apples and nuts. Spread in a greased pan and bake at 350° for 30-35 minutes. Cool and cut into squares.

Bake in a 9" x 13", 10" x 10", or 9" x 11" tin.

PUDDINGS

COTTAGE PUDDING

½ cup sugar
¼ cup butter or margarine
1 egg
1 teaspoon vanilla
1½ cups flour
1½ teaspoons baking powder
1/3 cup milk

Cream butter and sugar thoroughly. Add egg and beat well. Add vanilla and blend well. Alternately add flour and milk in small amounts. Beat until mixture is smooth. Pour into greased 8″ x 8″ pan. Bake at 400° for 20-25 minutes. Serve warm with lemon sauce or vanilla sauce.

LEMON SAUCE

½ cup sugar
1 tablespoon corn starch
1 cup water
2 tablespoons butter or margarine
½ teaspoon grated lemon rind
2 tablespoons lemon juice
Dash of salt

Combine sugar and corn starch. Gradually add water, stirring all the while. When the mixture is thickened add butter, lemon rind, lemon juice and salt. Beat well and serve over pudding.

LEMON CAKE PUDDING

¼ cup sifted all-purpose flour
1 cup sugar
¼ teaspoon salt
1½ teaspoon grated lemon rind
¼ cup lemon juice
2 egg yolks, well beaten
1 cup milk
2 egg whites, stiffly beaten

Heat oven to 350°. Sift dry ingredients into bowl. Stir in lemon rind, lemon juice, beaten egg yolks and milk. Mix well until all dry ingredients are moistened. Fold in beaten egg whites. Pour into 1-quart casserole and set in a pan of water enough to come halfway up around casserole. Bake for 40-50 minutes. Cake mixture will be at top and sauce at bottom of pudding.

This is very much like the lemon pudding in Mary Whitcher's cookbook. If you do not have fresh lemons, reconstituted lemon juice may be used with the same results.

INDIAN PUDDING

3 cups milk
¼ cup corn meal (I use yellow, although
    white is fine.)

¼ cup butter or margarine, cut into small pieces
½ cup molasses
½ teaspoon salt (*optional*)
½ teaspoon cinnamon
½ teaspoon ginger

In top of double boiler scald 2 cups milk. Very gradually stir in the corn meal. This must be done with care as it tends to lump. If it does lump, remove from boiling water and mix well until smooth. Use a beater if necessary. Stir over a simmering heat (high boil is too much cooking) for 10 minutes until it is smooth and thickened. Remove from heat and vigorously stir in butter until melted. Stir in remaining cup of milk, molasses, salt, ginger and cinnamon. Pour into buttered casserole and bake at 300° for 2 hours, or until pudding is reddish-brown and forms a crust. The center will be soft. Serve warm with whipped cream or ice cream.

OLD FASHIONED RICE PUDDING

1 cup water
½ cup long-grain rice
2½ cups milk
¼ cup raisins
2 eggs
¼ cup sugar, divided
½ teaspoon salt

1 teaspoon cinnamon
Butter or margarine (*optional*)

In double boiler, bring water to a boil. Stir in the rice. Cover and simmer for 15 minutes, or until all the water is absorbed. Stir in the milk. Cover, stirring occasionally, and cook for 45 minutes. Stir in the raisins and cook for 10 minutes, or until the rice is very soft. In a medium bowl beat eggs with 3 tablespoons sugar and salt. Stir a large spoonful of hot rice into egg mixture. Blend well, then mix egg mixture into the rice. Cook, stirring constantly, for a few minutes until mixture thickens slightly. Turn into serving bowls. Mix remaining tablespoon of sugar with cinnamon and sprinkle over the puddings. Serves 6.

TAPIOCA PUDDING

3 tablespoons instant or quick cooking tapioca
6 tablespoons sugar
3 cups milk
2 eggs, beaten
1 teaspoon vanilla
Dash of salt (*optional*)

Thoroughly mix beaten eggs with sugar. Add milk and blend until thoroughly mixed. Cook in top of double boiler until milk mixture is hot. Add tapioca stirring constantly until well blended. Continue to stir gently as mixture cooks for about 3 or 4 minutes.

Remove from heat. Add vanilla. Allow pudding to cool while covered.

This is good by itself, or it may have your choice of fruit, such as bananas added at the last moment before serving.

STRAWBERRY SUMMER PUDDING

½ loaf thin sliced white bread
1 quart ripe strawberries
¾ to 1 cup sugar (depending on the
   sweetness of the berries)

Remove crusts from bread. Mash and sweeten berries. Line pan or mold with foil or waxed paper. Place slices of bread on the bottom. Spoon mashed berries over the slices and alternate berries with bread until the pan is filled. Cover with waxed paper and cardboard cut slightly smaller than the pan and weight as evenly as possible. Chill at least 8 hours or overnight. For serving invert on a platter. Top with whipped cream and scatter fresh berries around pudding. Serves 6.

CREAM PUFFS

1 cup water
½ cup butter or margarine
1 cup flour
3 eggs

Put water and butter on to boil. When water boils stir in the flour. Remove from heat. When cool stir in eggs, one at a time, beating well after each egg. Drop from a spoon onto a greased pan and bake in a very hot oven, 450°, for 30 minutes. Cool and fill with filling below, pudding, whipped cream, or ice cream.

FILLING FOR CREAM PUFFS

½ cup sugar
½ teaspoon salt
2 cups good milk (not skim, but heavier)
4 egg yolks, or 2 eggs beaten
2 teaspoons vanilla

In a saucepan mix sugar, salt and flour. Stir in milk. Cook over low heat stirring constantly until it boils. Allow to boil for 1 or 2 minutes. Stir half of mixture into beaten eggs. Blend into the remaining hot mixture in saucepan. Cool and blend in vanilla.

For an interesting change use Shaker Rose Water in place of vanilla.

PLUM PUDDING

2 pounds raisins
½ pint wine, for plumping raisins
2 cups vegetable shortening or lard
12 eggs, separated
2 cups milk
½ cup maple syrup
8 cups flour
1½ teaspoons salt
1 teaspoon mace
1 teaspoon allspice
1 tablespoon cinnamon
1 tablespoon ginger

Plump raisins overnight in wine. Drain well, but reserve liquid. Cream the shortening. Add egg yolks to milk and maple syrup. Mix all dry ingredients together and combine everything except the egg whites, even the wine from the raisins. Beat egg whites and fold into mixture. Pour into a strong pudding bag which has been wetted and well dusted with flour. Do not tie too tightly for the pudding will swell. Plunge into a boiling pot and boil for 3 hours. Eat while still hot with custard sauce.

BROTHER TED'S CUSTARD SAUCE FOR PLUM PUDDING

2 eggs, beaten
1 cup sugar
½ pint heavy cream, whipped
2 egg whites, beaten stiff
½ teaspoon vanilla

Beat the 2 eggs and add the sugar. Continue to beat until creamy. Add in the whipped cream. Add vanilla and the egg whites which have been beaten until stiff. Fold until smooth.

This is delicious and we always eat much more sauce than pudding. We use it for Christmas and Thanksgiving dinners. The recipe was passed down from Brother Ted's mother.

This is especially good served over the Alfred Shaker Boiled Fruit Cake. The cake serves as an excellent plum pudding.

FLOATING ISLAND DESSERT

1 tablespoon corn starch
3 tablespoons sugar
Dash of salt
1 quart milk

5 eggs, separated
1 teaspoon vanilla or Shaker Rose Water

Mix and combine sugar, salt and corn starch. Beat egg yolks until lemon colored and thick. Add scalded milk to egg mixture. Then slowly add the first mixture to milk and egg. Stir constantly so as to have a smooth consistency. Cook over low heat, stirring constantly for 4-5 minutes. Add half of flavoring. Pour into individual serving dishes. Beat egg whites until very stiff and add salt, 2 tablespoons sugar and remainder of flavoring. Drop spoonfuls of egg white mixture into boiling water for about 2 minutes. Using a slotted spoon, remove and float on pudding. Add a tiny bit of stiff jelly to egg white.

Sister Della was fond of making this dessert. As children it was a great favorite of ours.

MOCHA RING DESSERT

1 cup very strong hot coffee
  (It can never be *too* strong, so if you like you may add 1 teaspoon instant coffee)
1 teaspoon gelatin
31 marshmallows
1 pint heavy cream, whipped

Remove ¼ cup of coffee and cool. In it dissolve the gelatin. In double boiler melt the marshmallows in the remaining hot coffee. Add dissolved gelatin. Whip ½ pint of cream and sweeten to taste. Unmold ring onto a platter. Heap whipped cream in center of ring. Garnish with shaved chocolate.

LEMON GRAPENUT PUDDING

1 cup sugar
4 tablespoons butter or margarine
1 teaspoon grated lemon rind
3 tablespoons lemon juice
2 eggs, separated
2 tablespoons flour
4 tablespoons grapenuts
1 cup milk

Cream together the sugar and butter. Add grated lemon rind. Beat egg yolks and add to the first mixture. Add lemon juice, flour, grapenuts and milk. Mix well after each addition. Beat egg whites until stiff. Fold the first mixture into beaten egg whites. Pour gently into baking dish. (I use a casserole dish.) Place dish in pan of hot water, allowing water to come halfway around baking dish. Bake at 325° for 1½ hours. When done it will have a sponge top and creamy pudding underneath.

ANGEL PUDDING

1½ cups fine soft bread crumbs
1 cup milk
2 eggs, separated
2 tablespoons butter or margarine
½ cup sugar
1½ teaspoons vanilla
1½ teaspoons grated lemon peel
½ teaspoon ground Shaker Coriander
¼ teaspoon ground cloves
½ cup finely chopped nuts
½ cup raisins
2 cups peeled chopped apples
Dash of salt

Combine bread crumbs and milk. Bring to a boil stirring constantly to prevent scorching. Cool. Add egg yolks, butter, sugar, vanilla, lemon peel, coriander and cloves to milk mixture. Beat well. Add nuts and raisins. Stir in apples. Beat egg whites and salt together until stiff. Fold into previous mixture. Bake in a greased 1-quart casserole dish at 375° for approximately 35 minutes. Serve while warm with cream.

CHERRY PUDDING

1 one-pound can water packed sour cherries
   (we use our own frozen cherries)
1 cup all-purpose flour

1 teaspoon baking soda
1 teaspoon cinnamon
½ teaspoon salt
¾ cup sugar
½ cup chopped nuts (*optional*)
1 egg
1 tablespoon butter or margarine, melted

Drain cherries, but reserve the juice for the sauce. Mix the next 6 ingredients together. Beat egg until thick and lemon colored. Add butter. Add the mixture and the cherries to the first mixture and mix all together until the dry ingredients are moistened. (No liquid is needed.) Spread in a greased shallow 1½ quart baking dish. Bake for 30 minutes at 375°. Cut into squares and serve with sauce.

SAUCE FOR CHERRY PUDDING

¼ cup sugar
1 tablespoon corn starch
1 cup cherry juice
   (*if not enough juice to make 1 cup, add enough water or fruit juice to make the cup of liquid. I sometimes use juice saved from jars of maraschino cherries for color.*)
1 tablespoon butter or margarine

Mix sugar and corn starch together in a small saucepan. Add the cherry juice and mix well. Cook stirring until smooth and thickened. Add butter and, if you desire, a drop or two of red food coloring. Serve hot over the pudding.

Our community likes a lot of sauce, so I always make extra.

BAKED APPLES

8 tart apples, the firmer the better
½ cup sugar
¼ teaspoon cinnamon
Lemon juice

Wash and core the apples. Mix together the sugar and cinnamon. Place apples in a buttered baking dish or a glass oven casserole may also be used. Fill centers of apples with sugar mixture. Add a little water to baking dish. Brush tops of apples with lemon juice. Bake in a 400° oven. Baste apples often with syrup which has formed in the dish. When apples are soft, but still firm, remove from the oven. Keep warm until ready to serve. Serve with whipped cream or a dash of ice cream sprinkled with sugar and cinnamon mixture.

APPLE CRISP

5 cups sliced apples
1 cup brown sugar
¾ cup flour
¾ cup cooking oatmeal
1 teaspoon cinnamon
½ cup butter or margarine

Arrange apple slices in a buttered baking pan, approximately 8″ x 8″ x 2″. Combine sugar, flour, oats and cinnamon until mixture is crumbly. Press mixture over apples. Bake at 350° for 45-50 minutes or until the top is browned. Serve warm with ice cream or whipped cream.

APPLE CRISP #2

¾ cup flour
½ cup firmly packed brown sugar (I prefer light brown sugar)
¼ teaspoon cinnamon
¼ pound butter or margarine
4 large apples, whatever is in season

In medium bowl combine flour, sugar and cinnamon. With a pastry blender cut in butter until very fine. Pare, core and thinly slice apples. Arrange apples in an 8″ square baking dish. Sprinkle flour mixture over apples. Bake at 450° for 30 minutes or until apples are tender and the top is browned. Serve warm with heavy cream, whipped cream or ice cream.

APPLE BROWN BETTY

½ cup sugar, brown or granulated
2/3 teaspoon cinnamon
½ teaspoon salt
3 cups coarse crumbled bread
6 apples, peeled and sliced
5 tablespoons melted butter or margarine

Combine the sugar, cinnamon and salt thoroughly. Cover bottom of a buttered pan or casserole with crumbs. Add a layer of sliced apples and sprinkle with sugar mixture. Repeat layers. Drizzle melted butter over all and cover. Bake at 375° for approximately 40 minutes. Uncover pan for the last 10 minutes. Serve with whipped cream or ice cream by itself. It is good any way. Serves 6.

I remember this recipe from years ago. Both Sister Ethel and Eldress Prudence were fond of making it.

APPLE BROWN BETTY #2

Peel and chop 6 apples. Place a layer of apples in a well buttered glass casserole. Add a layer of bread crumbs. Sprinkle with brown sugar and cinnamon. Repeat until the dish is filled. Add several generous dots of butter on top and pour sweet milk over all until it comes to within an inch of the top of dish.

Bake in a moderate oven, 350°, until brown and serve with ice cream.

This recipe was found in an old recipe book used by the Shakers years ago. I have tried it with good results. You may prefer the first recipe with the measured amounts.

ONE DISH APPLE PUDDING

2 eggs
1 cup sugar
3 tablespoons all-purpose flour
1 teaspoon baking powder
1 teaspoon vanilla or 1 teaspoon Shaker Rose Water
Dash of salt
¼ cup raisins
¼ cup finely chopped nuts (*optional*)
2 medium apples, peeled and finely diced
Plain cream, whipped cream, or ice cream

Break eggs into a 1½-quart casserole. Do not use a smaller dish as mixture rises and will go over the oven. Beat eggs well and then add all remaining ingredients except the cream. Bake in a 350° oven for approximately 35 minutes. If pudding doesn't look quite ready, allow another 10 minutes of baking. Serve warm with cream or ice cream. Makes 5 servings.

APPLE TAPIOCA CREAM

3 tablespoons instant tapioca (quick-setting tapioca
   is the same)
6 tablespoons sugar
1 teaspoon vanilla
3 cups milk
2 eggs
Pinch of salt
1 cup slightly sweetened applesauce

In top of double boiler heat milk until hot, but not
boiling. Beat eggs and combine with the sugar and
salt. Add to milk stirring until well mixed. Slowly
add tapioca to hot milk mixture stirring constantly
until thickened and smooth. This takes approximately
15 minutes. Remove from heat. Fold in applesauce
and vanilla. Serve warm or chilled, whichever is your
preference. This pudding is also good if you use 1
teaspoon Shaker Rose Water instead of vanilla.

VANILLA SAUCE #1

1 cup sugar
2 tablespoons corn starch
2 cups water
¼ cup butter or margarine
2 teaspoons vanilla
Dash of nutmeg (optional)

Combine sugar and corn starch. Slowly stir in water.
Boil for a few minutes stirring constantly. Stir in
butter, vanilla and nutmeg. Serve hot. Makes
approximately 2 cups.

VANILLA SAUCE #2

½ cup butter or margarine
1 cup sugar
½ cup light cream
1 teaspoon vanilla

Melt butter in medium saucepan. Remove from heat.
Add remaining ingredients, mixing well. Simmer,
stirring over low heat about 5 minutes or until the
sugar is dissolved. Serve hot over pudding or cake.

This recipe may also be used substituting Shaker Rose
Water for vanilla.

*Sister Ethel Peacock, also known as grandmother, was famous
for this type of dessert sauce.*

SPIRITUAL CAKE

As I have been informed of late,
There's something in the Shaker Cake
That does make souls contented here.
I'll now unfold the matter clear.
To all who have got eyes to see,
I will unveil this mystery ;
And tell them plainly how to make,
And feast upon the Shaker Cake.

'Tis called in Scripture " living bread,"
Because it quickens from the dead,
It saves the soul from sin and strife,
'Tis therefore called the " bread of life."
'Tis not much matter what's the name,
For lo ! in substance 'tis the same ;
Some call it cake with tempting seed,
'Tis that by which the soul is freed.

Though human wisdom cannot scan
How this supports the inner man ;
And while the soul is fed thereby,
A carnal nature has to die.
No earthly substance we employ,
But just our inward peace and joy,
Nor is it any natural yeast
That gives us this continual feast.

First, by an honest heart within.
Confessing and forsaking sin,
Gives us a taste of this good cake,
Thus hidden manna we partake.
'Tis seasoned with the seed of grace,
Which strengthens us to run the race ;
To quit all vain and earthly ties,
And run that we may win the prize.

And those who do all sin forsake,
May freely feast on this good cake ;
We know it is by heaven designed
Both to adorn and feast the mind.
It fills our souls with great delight,
Though 'tis to nature out of sight,
It is a substance we enjoy,
Which death and hell cannot destroy.

Whene'er enquirers come to see,
This cake is set before them free,
And if they love it, surely, they
Will quit their sins and want to stay.
But if the appetite is low,
The stomach must be cleansed, you know,
For while they in the broad way roam,
Their souls will loathe an honey-comb.

And when the system is made clean,
From all that's base or foul within,
They're able to discern the good,
And feast upon this heavenly food.
But if they slight this precious cake,
And our emetics will not take,
We give them up, if they refuse
To serve the master which they choose.

———

The foregoing hymn was composed by HANNAH
BROWNSON, a Shakeress, in consequence of a story
being in circulation that the Shakers put some kind
of seed into their cake which made those who partook
of it wish to remain among them.